YOU ARE THE STAR IN THE SKY OUR FATHER TOLD ABRAHAM ABOUT!

From Breaking Chains to Divine Order: A Prophetess' Guide to Healing, Freedom, and Power in Christ Jesus Name

FATHER, SON, HOLY-SPIRIT LET'S GO!

FEAST ON HIS PROMISES IN JESUS NAME

PROPHETESS SHERLINE OSCAR-MARCELLUS

FROM BREAKING CHAINS TO DIVINE ORDER

A Prophetess Guide to Healing, Freedom, and Power in Christ Jesus Name.

Sherline Oscar-Marcellus

Copyright © Sherline Oscar-Marcellus

All rights reserved.

No part of this publication may be reproduced, stored in a retrieval system, or transmitted in any form or by any means: electronic, mechanical, photocopying, recording, or otherwise without the prior written permission of the author, except in the case of brief quotations used in articles or reviews.

CONTENTS

INTRODUCTION	11
THE WOUNDS WE CARRY	13
THE ENEMY'S TRAP	24
THE LIE OF STAYING BROKEN	39
GOD, THE ONLY TRUE RESTORER	52
POWER OVER DARKNESS	62
THE PATH OF HEALING THROUGH THE FATHER, THE SON AND THE HOLY SPIRIT	73
BECOMING YOUR BEST SELF IN CHRIST	91
HELPING OTHERS HEAL	104
LIVING IN DIVINE OR BECOMING YOUR BEST SELF IN CHRIST WITH THE HOLY SPIRIT	112
CONCLUSION	116
PROPHETIC PRAYERS FOR EACH CHAPTER	118
PROPHETIC DECLARATIONS FOR EACH CHAPTERS	121
THANKSGIVING PRAYER	127

ABOUT THE AUTHOR

Hey Its Prophetess S.O.M, and I have witnessed firsthand the power of the Holy-Spirit over darkness — including witches, warlocks, and spiritual attacks — and I want to guide others into the same freedom in Jesus Name.

As a Prophetess, I'm eager to witness you rise from brokenness into being your best self, anchored in God's TRUTH now and Forevermore..A Journey from Pain to Purpose Through the Only True Power — FATHER,SON, and the HOLY SPIRIT!Childhood trauma may break or wound us, but it does not define our destiny .

Holy-Spirit is the only one who can truly restore, heal, and bring divine order.

Coming against witches, warlocks, and dark powers **WITH THE POWER OF THE HOLY SPIRIT.**

FATHER, SON, HOLY SPIRIT LETS GO!

By the authority of this believer in Christ Jesus name this is the reason for the book

Her Testimony: Childhood Trauma, My Calling as a Prophetess, and why I'm writing this book. You are the STAR he told Abraham about!

*Understanding Childhood Trauma

*What it is, and how it shapes lives

*Emotional, mental, and spiritual effects

*The Lie of Staying Broken

*How the enemy uses pain to keep us bound.

*Why trauma doesn't have to define you.

*Holy-Spirit, the Only True Restorer

*Scriptures on healing and restoration.

*Understanding divine order in your life.

*Spiritual Warfare and Deliverance

*Walking the Path of Healing

*Practical steps of healing (prayer, counseling, forgiveness, self-discipline)

*How to align with Kingdom plans daily.

*Becoming Your Best Self in Christ with the Holy-Spirit

*Purpose, identity, and calling after trauma.

*Building resilience and a life of joy.

*Helping Others Heal

*How your healing equips you to help others.

*Testimony as a weapon against the enemy.

*Rising Above for God's Glory

*Prayer of restoration and empowerment.

THE LORD's COVENANT WITH ABRAM GENESIS 15
FULL CHAPTER

1 After this, the word of the LORD came to Abram in a vision:

"Do not be afraid, Abram. I am your shield,[a]

your very great reward.[b]"

2 But Abram said, "Sovereign LORD, what can you give me since I remain childless and the one who will inherit[c] my estate is Eliezer of Damascus?"

3 And Abram said, "You have given me no children; so a servant in my household will be my heir."

4 Then the word of the LORD came to him: "This man will not be your heir, but a son who is your own flesh and blood will be your heir."

5 He took him outside and said, "Look up at the sky and count the stars—if indeed you can count them." Then he said to him, "So shall your offspring[d] be."

6 Abram believed the LORD, and he credited it to him as righteousness.

7 He also said to him, "I am the LORD, who brought you out of Ur of the Chaldeans to give you this land to take possession of it."

8 But Abram said, "Sovereign LORD, how can I know that I will gain possession of it?"

9 So the LORD said to him, "Bring me a heifer, a goat and a ram, each three years old, along with a dove and a young pigeon."

10 Abram brought all these to him, cut them in two and arranged the halves opposite each other; the birds, however, he did not cut in half.

11 Then birds of prey came down on the carcasses, but Abram drove them away.

12 As the sun was setting, Abram fell into a deep sleep, and a thick and dreadful darkness came over him.

13 Then the LORD said to him, "Know for certain that for four hundred years your descendants will be strangers in a country not their own and that they will be enslaved and mistreated there

14 But I will punish the nation they serve as slaves, and afterward they will come out with great possessions.

15 You, however, will go to your ancestors in peace and be buried at a good old age.

16 In the fourth generation your descendants will come back here, for the sin of the Amorites has not yet reached its full measure.

17 When the sun had set and darkness had fallen, a smoking firepot with a blazing torch appeared and passed between the pieces.

18 On that day the LORD made a covenant with Abram and said, "To your descendants I give this land, from the Wadi[e] of Egypt to the great river, the Euphrates—

19 the land of the Kenites, Kenizzites, Kadmonites,

20 Hittites, Perizzites, Rephaites,

21 Amorites, Canaanites, Girgashites and Jebusites."

INTRODUCTION

There are moments in life that leave scars so deep, they seem impossible to heal. Childhood trauma is one of them. It has a way of shaping how we see ourselves, how we love, how we trust, and how we walk through life. For many, it feels like the pain will always speak louder than the promise of who they were created to be.

But I am here to tell you: you do not have to stay broken.

I know what it is to be crushed by pain, to carry the weight of wounds from childhood into adulthood. I know what it feels like to be silenced, overlooked, or used. But I also know what it means to be restored by the three in One who can truly heal—Father, Son and the Hoy Spirit..

I did not write this book to glorify trauma. I wrote it to glorify the Father, Son and The Holy Spirit. .Only they can take the shattered pieces of a life and make it whole again. They can silence the voice of the enemy, cancel the assignments of witches and warlocks, and lift us into our rightful place as children of light.

As a prophetess, I have walked in spiritual warfare. I have seen firsthand that the battles we face are not just physical or emotional—they are spiritual.

The enemy would love for you to stay blind, but Through these pages, I will share not only my story, but the truths the 3 in 1 has revealed to me. Together, we will walk through the reality of trauma, the necessity of healing, and the power of deliverance. And by the end, my prayer is that you will not just read my testimony—you will rise into your own understanding of your spiritual life.

Because when God restores, He doesn't just put you back together. He makes you new.

Welcome to your journey of healing, freedom, and divine order with Father, Son and the Holy Spirit.

Scripture anchor: "The Spirit of the Lord is upon me, because He has anointed me to heal the brokenhearted…" (Luke 4:18).

Chapter 1

THE WOUNDS WE CARRY

Identifying The Wounds We Carry

Physical Abuse: Intentional infliction of physical harm, such as hitting, kicking, burning, or restraining. Sexual Abuse: Any form of sexual contact with a child, including molestation, rape, or exposure to pornography.

Emotional Abuse: Verbal or non-verbal actions that damage a child's sense of self-worth, such as humiliation, rejection, or isolation. Neglect: Failure to provide for a child's basic needs, such as food, shelter, clothing, medical care, or supervision. Witnessing Violence: Observing acts of violence, such as domestic violence, community violence, or war.

Loss of a Loved One: Experiencing the death of a significant person in their life, such as a parent, sibling, or friend. Disasters and Accidents: Witnessing or experiencing major events, such as natural disasters, accidents, or terrorist attacks. Complex Trauma: Repeated exposure to multiple traumatic events, often in a chronic or ongoing manner.

Adverse Childhood Experiences, or ACEs, is a term developed by the CDC and Kaiser Permanente to cover many traumatic events and conditions that children might face. High ACE scores are associated with an increased risk of health problems, mental illness, and substance abuse in adulthood.

ACEs are categorized into three areas:

- **Abuse:** This can include physical, emotional, and sexual abuse. Neglect: Both emotional and physical neglect are considered ACEs. Household challenges: These include substance use, mental illness, or domestic violence within the home.

- **Single-incident trauma:** This type of trauma results from a single event that is frightening, violent, or life-threatening. The experience can affect a child who witnessed or was directly involved in the event.

- **Medical trauma:** This involves a child's psychological and physiological response to a serious illness, painful medical procedures, or frightening treatments. Natural and man-made disasters: Traumatic events like fires, floods, earthquakes, car accidents, school shootings, or terrorist acts. Loss: The sudden or violent death of a close friend or family member can be traumatic.

Complex trauma describes exposure to multiple, chronic, and pervasive traumatic events, often of an interpersonal nature. Because complex trauma often happens within the child's caregiving system (e.g., in their home), it can disrupt their ability to form healthy attachments and regulate emotions.

Examples of complex trauma include: Prolonged physical, sexual, or emotional abuse, Chronic neglect, Witnessing ongoing domestic violence, Parental substance abuse or mental illness, Repeated separation from a primary caregiver.

Developmental Trauma (DT) or Developmental Trauma Disorder (DTD) describes severe and cumulative interpersonal trauma that disrupts a child's development during sensitive periods. It is often tied to insecure attachment with caregivers and can cause long-lasting effects on a child's emotional, physical, and cognitive abilities. DTD is often used interchangeably with complex trauma, although DTD has not been officially recognized as a diagnosis in the DSM-5.

Other Forms of Childhood Trauma

- **Community violence:** Witnessing or experiencing violence in the community, such as gang activity or riots.Refugee trauma: Trauma experienced by refugee children, including war-related events, displacement, and the challenges of resettlement.Bullying: Being a repeated victim of unprovoked physical or psychological harm.

-

- **Racial trauma:** Experiencing racism, prejudice, and discrimination can have traumatic effects on a child's sense of safety and self-worth.

The emotional scars of childhood trauma can profoundly affect an individual's life well into adulthood. Since the child's brain and nervous system are still developing, traumatic experiences can disrupt emotional growth and alter how they relate to others and see themselves. These invisible wounds can affect mental health, relationships, and even physical well-being.

Mental and emotional effects of Childhood Trauma

- **Anxiety and depression:** Unresolved trauma is a major risk factor for developing anxiety disorders and depression later in life. The constant state of fear and alertness during childhood can create a pervasive sense of unease.

- **Emotional dysregulation:** Trauma can make it difficult for adults to identify, manage, and tolerate their feelings. This can lead to intense mood swings, angry outbursts, or emotional numbness.

- **Low self-esteem and shame:** Children who experience emotional neglect or abuse may internalize the belief that they are unworthy, unloved, or to blame. These feelings of inadequacy and worthlessness can persist throughout life.

- **Dissociation:** Dissociation is a defense mechanism in which the mind disconnects from reality to escape overwhelming pain. In adulthood, survivors may continue to dissociate, leading to memory gaps, a sense of detachment from oneself or surroundings, and an unstable sense of self.

- **Complex PTSD:** This can develop from chronic, repeated trauma and includes standard PTSD symptoms along with a distorted self-concept, difficulty with emotional regulation, and significant relationship problems.

Relationship challenges from Childhood Trauma

- **Difficulty trusting others:** When trust is broken during childhood, it becomes difficult to form safe and trusting relationships with others later in life. Trauma survivors may push people away or struggle with intense jealousy and a fear of abandonment.

- **Insecure attachment styles:** Trauma, especially neglect or abuse, can disrupt a child's attachment to their caregivers, leading to insecure attachment styles (anxious, avoidant, or disorganized) in adulthood. These patterns influence how adults form and navigate relationships.

- **Dysfunctional relationship patterns:** Trauma survivors may repeat unhealthy patterns from their childhood. For example, they might be drawn to emotionally unavailable partners or self-sabotage healthy relationships.

They may also be hypervigilant for red flags and quick to end a relationship at the first sign of conflict.

- **People-pleasing:** A child who grew up constantly trying to gain approval from an abusive or neglectful caregiver may develop people-pleasing tendencies in adulthood. They may go to great lengths to please others, often at the expense of their own needs.

Behavioral and Physical Effects

- **Self-destructive behaviors:** Some individuals may develop unhealthy coping mechanisms, such as substance abuse, to numb emotional pain. This can be a way to self-soothe when emotional regulation skills were never learned.

- **Overwhelming stress response:** Trauma can disrupt the body's stress response system, leading to chronic physical symptoms like headaches, stomachaches, and chronic pain. It can also increase the risk of chronic health conditions like heart disease, obesity, and autoimmune disorders later in life.

- **Sleep disturbances:** The heightened state of alertness associated with trauma can lead to insomnia, nightmares, or night terrors.

- **Compulsive behaviors:** Unprocessed trauma can lead to trauma-blocking behaviors like workaholism, compulsive internet use, or emotional eating as a way to avoid painful memories and emotions.

How Trauma Distorts Identity

Fragmentation of self Traumatic experiences can cause an individual's sense of self to break into disconnected parts, a process known as dissociation.

To survive chronic distress, a child may disconnect from their emotions, memories, and even their body. This can result in:

1. A feeling of having "missing parts" of oneself.

2. A disjointed or "fractured" identity, leading to feelings of confusion about who they are.

3. Developing a "false self" to cope with abuse or neglect, masking their vulnerability to gain acceptance from a caregiver.

Distorted self-worth

Trauma often leads survivors to internalize negative messages, creating a deep-seated belief that they are fundamentally flawed, unlovable, or worthless.

This can manifest in several ways:

- **Shame and guilt:** A child may blame themselves for the trauma, believing they were responsible for the abuse or neglect.

- **Low self-esteem:** This can lead to a constant need for external validation and approval, as a person feels they cannot be "good enough" on their own.

- **People-pleasing:** The drive to earn love and acceptance can result in being overly self-sacrificing or unable to advocate for one's own needs.

Re-Orienting Around Trauma

In some cases, the trauma can become the defining moment of a person's life, preventing them from developing an identity separate from their pain.

Identity is formed through a "coherent narrative" of one's life, and trauma can hijack this narrative.

- **Over-identification**: The individual's entire life story can become centered on their experience as a trauma survivor.
- **Repetition of traumatic dynamics:** A person may unconsciously recreate unhealthy dynamics in new situations, reinforcing their role as a victim or a survivor in need of protection.

How Trauma Distorts Relationships

Insecure attachment styles

Trauma, especially when inflicted by a primary caregiver, disrupts the development of secure attachment, where a child learns that others can be trusted to meet their needs. This can lead to insecure attachment styles that carry into adulthood.

- **Anxious attachment:** Characterized by a fear of abandonment, leading to clinginess, possessiveness, or a constant need for reassurance.

- **Avoidant attachment:** Characterized by a deep fear of intimacy, causing emotional distancing, a fierce sense of independence, and difficulty with vulnerability.

- **Disorganized attachment:** A mixture of anxious and avoidant traits that leads to a push-pull dynamic. The person craves closeness but is terrified of it, often due to inconsistent or abusive caregiving in childhood.

Difficulty With Trust and Intimacy

Because trauma teaches a person that the world and other people are not safe, trust can be fundamentally broken.

Hypervigilance: Trauma survivors may remain on high alert for perceived threats, making it difficult to relax and trust in a relationship.

Isolation: The inability to trust can lead to withdrawal and social isolation, making it difficult to form close bonds.

Trauma bonding: This is an intense emotional attachment to an abuser or dysfunctional dynamic, fueled by cycles of abuse and kindness.

Communication Challenges and Emotional Dysregulation

Trauma can hinder a person's ability to express and manage their emotions in a healthy way.

Emotional reactivity: Survivors may have a hair-trigger response to perceived threats, leading to intense and disproportionate emotional reactions in arguments.

Numbing: Alternatively, a person may shut down emotionally during conflicts, creating distance and frustration for their partner.

Communication breakdown: The combination of emotional dysregulation and mistrust can lead to miscommunication, with one person feeling unheard and the other feeling unsafe.

Healing the Distortions

It's important to remember that these distortions are survival mechanisms, not inherent flaws. They are adaptations that help a child cope with an unpredictable or threatening environment. Healing is possible through self-awareness and intentional work, often with the guidance of a professional.

Effective approaches to healing and rebuilding include:

- **Therapy:** Modalities like Trauma-Focused Cognitive Behavioral Therapy (TF-CBT), Eye Movement Desensitization and Reprocessing (EMDR), and Internal Family Systems (IFS) can help process a sense of safety and control.

- **Building self-worth:** Practicing self-compassion and challenging negative self-perceptions is crucial for healing. Choosing safe trauma.

- **Developing healthy boundaries:** Learning to assert personal limits helps restore relationships: With increased awareness, a trauma survivor can learn to choose partners who exhibit consistency, respect, and clear communication.

A wound is not the same as a death—it can heal. The Father.Son and the Holy-Spirit wants to heal you! Accept your healing today in Jesus name.

Man in the Mirror Questions: Father, Son and the Holy-Spirit What childhood wounds are still shaping me?

Chapter 2

THE ENEMY'S TRAP

Trauma as a tool of the enemy to keep people bound.

Some theological and spiritual traditions view trauma as a tool the "enemy" or evil forces use to inflict spiritual bondage, control, and separation from the kingdom of the trinity. This perspective does not replace psychological understanding of trauma but rather works alongside it, seeing psychological and spiritual issues as interwoven.

How Trauma Can be Used as a Spiritual Tool of Bondage

Within this framework, trauma creates vulnerabilities that can be exploited by evil forces to keep a person spiritually, emotionally, and relationally "bound" or imprisoned. Creates spiritual "open doors":

Traumatic events, such as abuse, violence, or betrayal, can wound a person's soul and leave them vulnerable to demonic influence or oppression. In this view, the initial trauma may not be the person's fault, but it can create an access point for evil spirits to harass and torment them long after the event has passed.

- **Perpetuates cycles of sin:** Some traditions believe that persistent, unhealed trauma can open the door to spirits of sin, such as addiction, lust, or rage. This can perpetuate destructive patterns and keep an individual stuck in a cycle of hurt and self-destructive behavior.

- **Encourages agreement with lies:** Trauma can lead individuals to internalize lies about themselves, others, and the Kingdom of trinity. An individual might believe they are worthless, unforgivable, or that God cannot be trusted. The enemy is seen as using these lies to keep a person in spiritual bondage and isolation.

- **Distorts identity in Christ:** The spiritual enemy can use trauma to define a person by their past experiences rather than their identity as a treasured child of God. This distortion can lead to confusion, shame, and a sense of disconnection from their true purpose.

- **Creates unforgiveness and bitterness:** Trauma can make it incredibly difficult to forgive those who have caused harm. The enemy can exploit this unforgiveness to fuel bitterness, resentment, and a desire for revenge, which further binds a person emotionally and spiritually.

- **Promotes isolation:** Evil forces can use fear and mistrust, which are common results of trauma, to isolate a person from healthy community, supportive relationships, and closeness with the Kingdom of Trinity. The isolation reinforces the feeling of being alone and makes healing more difficult.

Healing and Freedom

For those who adopt this spiritual perspective, healing requires addressing both the psychological and spiritual dimensions of trauma. Approaches to achieve spiritual freedom may include:

Deliverance ministry: This involves casting out evil spirits that may have gained access through unhealed trauma.

Forgiveness: Actively choosing to forgive offenders is seen as a way to close the door to spiritual torment caused by bitterness and resentment.

Inner healing: This involves inviting Jesus to go back to the traumatic event and speak truth and peace into that painful memory, helping to remove the associated emotional pain and replace lies with truth.

Renewing the mind: This is the practice of consciously replacing traumatic thought patterns and lies with the truth found in Scripture.

Counseling: Pairing spiritual care with professional trauma-informed therapy is often recommended for comprehensive healing.

Building healthy relationships: Connecting with others in a safe and loving community can help counteract the effects of isolation and mistrust caused by trauma.

Cycles of pain: Generational Curses, Repeated Patterns

Exodus 34:7 NLT

I lavish unfailing love to a thousand generations. I forgive iniquity, rebellion, and sin. But I do not excuse the guilty. I lay the sins of the parents upon their children and grandchildren; the entire family is affected— even children in the third and fourth generations."

"Cycles of pain" in families, often referred to as generational curses or generational trauma, are dysfunctional patterns of behavior, coping, and relating that are passed down through family lines.

The term "generational curse" is often used in spiritual contexts to describe repeated misfortunes or negative traits rooted in sin or unaddressed family trauma.

"Generational trauma" or "intergenerational trauma" is the psychological term for this phenomenon, explaining how the effects of trauma extend beyond the individual and influence subsequent generations.

This cycle can be perpetuated through various pathways, including learned behaviors, psychological transmission, and, according to emerging research, epigenetic inheritance.

Common Patterns in Cycles of Pain

Repeated family patterns that indicate inherited trauma can include:

Recurring emotional issues: Persistent and unexplained anxiety, depression, anger, or shame that seems to have no clear cause in an individual's current life.

Dysfunctional coping mechanisms: Cycles of substance abuse, self-harm, or emotional withdrawal used to numb emotional pain across generations.

Relationship difficulties: Repeating patterns of divorce, infidelity, codependency, or unhealthy attachment styles that undermine trust and intimacy.

Emotional suppression: A family culture where expressing emotions is discouraged or punished, creating an atmosphere of silence around painful experiences.

Hypervigilance: A heightened state of alertness and anxiety, often inherited from ancestors who lived in unsafe or oppressive environments, like those in war or slavery.

Physical ailments: In some cases, the chronic stress from generational trauma can manifest as unexplained physical symptoms like chronic pain, digestive issues, or fatigue.

How the Cycle is Perpetuated

This transmission of pain is not intentional but rather an unconscious process driven by unhealed wounds.

Learned behaviors: Children observe how their parents and other family members respond to stress and emotional challenges. For instance, if a parent who grew up with abuse resorts to yelling, their children are more likely to adopt this as a coping strategy.

Impacted parenting styles: Parents with unresolved trauma may struggle with emotional regulation and healthy attachment, which affects how they raise their children. This can result in emotionally distant, overly strict, or inconsistent parenting.

Sociological and collective trauma: Large-scale traumatic events like war, systemic oppression, or forced migration can create enduring collective trauma. The survival mechanisms adopted by the traumatized community become ingrained in the culture and passed down through generations, often as a fearful or distrustful outlook on life.

Epigenetic inheritance: Scientific studies have found that trauma can create molecular "tags" on a person's genes that can be passed down.

These changes can alter how genes are expressed, potentially making future generations more susceptible to stress and mental health issues.

Steps Toward Breaking the Cycle

Breaking a generational cycle of pain is a challenging but possible journey.

- **Acknowledge and identify the patterns:** The first and most crucial step is to recognize that a cycle exists. This can involve creating a genogram, a visual family tree that maps out recurring emotional and behavioral patterns across generations.

- **Seek therapeutic intervention:** Professional help, such as trauma-informed therapy or Eye Movement Desensitization and Reprocessing (EMDR), can provide a safe space to explore and process the root causes of the trauma.

- **Develop self-awareness and self-care:** Practices like mindfulness, journaling, or regular self-reflection help individuals recognize their triggers and responses, enabling them to choose different actions rather than react instinctively.

- **Foster open communication:** Gently but honestly discussing family history and traumatic experiences can break the cycle of silence and shame that often surrounds generational trauma.

- **Cultivate spiritual resilience (for those who seek it):** For people with spiritual beliefs, practices like prayer, forgiveness, and deliverance ministry are seen as tools to overcome spiritual bondage associated with curses.

- **Choose a new narrative:** By intentionally making different choices from previous generations and creating new, healthier family traditions, individuals can begin to build a legacy of healing and resilience for those who come after them.

Introduction to spiritual warfare: the devil exploits trauma to plant lies.

Some theological and spiritual perspectives describe spiritual warfare as a battle between good and evil, where the "enemy," often referred to as the devil or Satan, exploits personal weaknesses to deceive and bind people. In this framework, trauma is seen as a key point of entry for the enemy to plant lies, which can lead to spiritual and emotional distress long after the initial traumatic event has occurred.

How Trauma Provides an Opening

From a spiritual warfare perspective, trauma can create an opening in a person's life that evil forces can exploit.

Emotional wounds: Trauma often wounds a person's soul, leaving behind emotional scars like fear, shame, and feelings of worthlessness. The enemy to amplify these feelings to create torment.

Overwhelmed defenses: Traumatic events can overwhelm a person's natural coping mechanisms, much like "deflector shields being down". This makes them vulnerable to spiritual attacks, with spirits of fear being among the most common.

Distorted perception of God: Trauma can alter a person's view of a higher power. It might cause them to feel abandoned or punished by God, or to question how a loving God could allow such suffering.

Isolation: The enemy thrives on isolating the injured and vulnerable. Trauma can cause people to withdraw from healthy relationships and community, leaving them disconnected from the support systems that could provide truth and healing.

Lies the Enemy plants During and After Trauma

For though we walk in the flesh, we do not war according to the flesh. For the weapons of our warfare are not carnal but mighty in God for pulling down strongholds, casting down arguments and every high thing that exalts itself against the knowledge of God, bringing every thought into captivity to the obedience of Christ, and being ready to punish all disobedience when your obedience is fulfilled.

The enemy is considered the "father of lies" and specializes in twisting truth to create spiritual bondage. Trauma creates a fertile ground for these lies to take root. Some lies the enemy plants in us. Things like"I am worthless and unlovable", "My life has no purpose", "I am fundamentally flawed and will never be fixed". Lies about others, "People are selfish and will always hurt me", "It's every man for himself, so I can't trust anyone","If I get close to someone, I will be hurt". Lies about God, "God is not good, or He would have prevented this". "God has abandoned me in my time of need","I've sinned too much, and God won't forgive me".

Combating the Lies and Healing From Trauma

1 "Let not your heart be troubled; you believe in God, believe also in Me.

2 In My Father's house are many mansions; if it were not so, I would have told you. I go to prepare a place for you.

3 And if I go and prepare a place for you, I will come again and receive you to Myself; that where I am, there you may be also.

4 And where I go you know, and the way you know."

5 Thomas said to Him, "Lord, we do not know where You are going, and how can we know the way?"

6 Jesus said to him, "I am the way, the truth, and the life. No one comes to the Father except through Me.

7 "If you had known Me, you would have known My Father also; and from now on you know Him and have seen Him." - John 14:1-7 NKJV

Addressing this spiritual dimension of trauma involves actively fighting the lies with spiritual truth.

Expose the lie to the light: Just as a counselor might challenge a false belief, spiritually, one must expose the enemy's lies to the light of Christ to break their power.

Inner healing: This practice involves inviting God into the traumatic memory to bring peace and reveal His perspective.

Replace lies with truth: Actively using scripture to counter the lies planted by trauma is a key weapon in spiritual warfare. For example, replacing the lie "I am unlovable" with God's truth that "I am a treasured child of God".

Forgiveness: Releasing forgiveness to offenders is seen as a way to shut the door to bitterness and spiritual torment.

Deliverance: For some, freedom from the spiritual effects of trauma involves receiving deliverance from oppressive spirits.

Combine with therapy: Many who hold this view advocate for a holistic approach that pairs spiritual practices with professional trauma-informed therapy.

Warning: *Witches, Warlocks, and Demonic Forces Target the Brokenhearted because They are Vulnerable*

25 At that time Jesus answered and said, "I thank You, Father, Lord of heaven and earth, that You have hidden these things from the wise and prudent and have revealed them to babes.

26 Even so, Father, for so it seemed good in Your sight.

27 All things have been delivered to Me by My Father, and no one knows the Son except the Father. Nor does anyone know the Father except the Son, and the one to whom the Son wills to reveal Him.

28 Come to Me, all you who labor and are heavy laden, and I will give you rest.

29 Take My yoke upon you and learn from Me, for I am gentle and lowly in heart, and you will find rest for your souls.

30 For My yoke is easy and My burden is light. - Matthew 11:25-30

From a spiritual warfare perspective, individuals suffering from trauma and heartbreak are seen as particularly vulnerable to attacks from malevolent spiritual forces. This viewpoint, held by various spiritual and theological traditions, suggests that emotional and psychological wounds can create "open doors" or weaknesses that the enemy—referred to as the devil, witches, warlocks, or demonic forces—can exploit. The ultimate goal of such attacks is to plant lies, isolate the individual, and keep them from spiritual healing.

Why the Brokenhearted are Seen as Vulnerable

Trauma and heartbreak are believed to create specific vulnerabilities that make a person susceptible to spiritual influence:

Weakened defenses: Emotional pain and exhaustion deplete a person's energy and spiritual defenses, leaving them less able to resist negative spiritual influences.

Intense negative emotions: Intense feelings like despair, bitterness, shame, and fear can be amplified by demonic forces to create overwhelming spiritual oppression.

Isolation: The enemy often works to isolate the traumatized and heartbroken, as loneliness and disconnection from supportive communities make individuals easier targets.

Distorted perception of God: Trauma can cause a person to question God's love and goodness, which the enemy can use to sow doubt and create a spiritual division.

Tactics Used to Exploit Vulnerability

The enemy, from a spiritual warfare standpoint, employs specific tactics to target the emotionally wounded.

Planting lies: The enemy, the "father of lies," can implant thoughts that amplify the trauma. Examples include lies like "I am worthless," "I am unlovable," or "This was my fault". These untruths align with the shame and low self-worth often caused by trauma.

Discouragement and weariness: Attacks can come in successive "stings," building on past wounds to overwhelm and discourage an individual to the point of despair. This can manifest as fatigue and a loss of spiritual desire.

Exacerbating mental distress: The enemy can exploit psychological vulnerabilities that arise from trauma, such as anxiety, intrusive thoughts, and emotional turmoil. While these are real mental health issues, this perspective suggests they can be exacerbated by spiritual forces.

Promoting unforgiveness: Holding onto resentment and bitterness toward those who caused the initial trauma is seen as a "foothold" for the enemy.

Unforgiveness is believed to poison the soul and block the path to healing.

Spiritual Countermeasures

For those who believe they are under such attack, spiritual countermeasures are recommended to find protection and healing.

Identify and resist lies: Actively discerning and challenging the enemy's lies by replacing them with spiritual truth is a powerful defense.

Rely on spiritual authority: The belief that spiritual authority in Christ can command the demonic realm to flee is a core component of this worldview.

Engage in prayer and community: Prayer, especially when done with a supportive community, is considered a vital spiritual weapon. Seeking out safe, healthy relationships helps break the isolation the enemy fosters.

Forgiveness: Pursuing forgiveness, even when difficult, is seen as a critical step to close the door to bitterness and further spiritual torment.

Seek inner healing: The spiritual practice of inviting divine intervention to heal traumatic memories and emotional wounds is key to resolving the underlying trauma that the enemy is exploiting.

Combine spiritual and clinical care: Many faith-based counselors and spiritual leaders advocate for a holistic approach, combining spiritual disciplines with professional, trauma-informed therapy.

Scripture Anchor: *"The thief comes only to steal, kill, and destroy; I have come that they may have life…" (John 10:10).*

Chapter 3

THE LIE OF STAYING BROKEN

When someone has experienced trauma, especially in childhood, society can send powerful messages that reinforce a fixed, damaged identity, rather than one capable of growth and healing. This can come from direct statements or more subtle, systemic biases. This can prevent individuals from seeking help and make it more difficult for them to move beyond their past.

Direct Societal Messaging and Stigma

Society often reacts to trauma survivors in ways that reinforce a damaged or fundamentally different identity. "This is just who you are now." When people define you by your past trauma, it can feel as if your identity is permanently tainted. Comments like "you'll never be good enough" or "this is what a person from a broken home is like" suggest that the trauma is the final chapter of your story.

Dismissal and minimizing: Some people may minimize emotional trauma that isn't sexual or physical, implying it wasn't a "true trauma" and that your emotional responses are unwarranted. This can lead to survivors feeling shame and silencing their pain, thinking, "I'm fine. Other people have it so much worse".

A "fixed mindset" toward mental illness: Public stigma often frames mental health conditions like PTSD and depression as permanent flaws rather than treatable conditions. Studies show that people exposed to "fixed mindset" messages on social media feel that mental illness is more stable and innate.

Systemic and Cultural Influences

The idea that trauma is a permanent state is also upheld by larger systems and cultural beliefs.

Reinforced social exclusion: Childhood trauma is linked to an increased likelihood of social exclusion in adulthood. Systemic trauma, such as discrimination and poverty, can erode trust in institutions and lead to isolation and fewer opportunities for those affected.

Stigma and discrimination: Survivors with "concealable stigmatized identities"—such as a history of mental illness or abuse—can face prejudice and discrimination from others if their past is revealed. This fear of rejection can cause individuals to hide their true experiences, reinforcing a sense of being "damaged goods".

Distorted public narratives: Media and cultural narratives can misrepresent or oversimplify what trauma is. While awareness has grown, some people use "trauma" as a "cultural touchstone" without understanding its full meaning, which can invalidate the experiences of true survivors.

Internalizing the Message

These societal messages can be powerful enough to be internalized, influencing a person's self-perception.

Trauma as a core identity: Trauma can become so central to an individual's life story that it becomes their defining trait. The person's identity is constructed through the lens of their traumatic experience, sometimes in a way that is "unsuccessful" and leads to further distress.

Identity distress: The unresolved issues from trauma can manifest as worry and anxiety about one's self-concept, leading to identity distress and making it difficult to form a coherent sense of self.

Self-sabotage: Believing that you are permanently broken can lead to self-destructive behaviors and an inability to maintain healthy relationships, which only confirms the false belief that "this is just who you are".

Overcoming the Societal Narrative.

It is important to remember that this societal narrative is a lie. Healing and post-traumatic growth are possible.

Trauma-informed care: Trauma-informed approaches in mental health and community settings can help individuals challenge these internal and external messages and reclaim a healthy, non-trauma-based identity.

Building a new narrative: Healing involves telling a new story—one that acknowledges the trauma but does not allow it to define the future. This includes focusing on resilience, growth, and empowerment.

Connecting with support: Finding supportive relationships and communities, both personal and professional, can counteract the social isolation and stigma that reinforce a "permanent" identity of trauma.

Why Self-Help Without God is Limited.

From a faith-based perspective, self-help methods alone are often considered limited because they focus on human effort and inner strength while overlooking a spiritual dimension. A Christian worldview, in particular, suggests that true and lasting transformation comes from a relationship with the trinity, not from self-improvement alone.

Here are several reasons why self-help without God is seen as limited: It cannot address the heart! Many Christian and spiritual traditions believe that the deepest human problems are spiritual at their core. While self-help can offer practical tips for changing behavior, it cannot fundamentally transform a person's heart or motives. This is because: A "self-centered gospel" is limited. Self-help literature and techniques are founded on human effort, resolve, and discipline. The Gospel, by contrast, is centered on Christ and our dependence on him.

The heart is the source of our problems. The Bible indicates that our desires, thoughts, and actions flow from the heart. Trying to fix behavior without addressing the underlying heart issue is seen as treating the symptoms instead of the cause.

It Fails Under the Heaviest Burdens

Self-help's reliance on willpower is often seen as inadequate in the face of profound suffering, chronic issues, or deeply ingrained sin. Pain shatters illusions of self-reliance. When we experience immense pain, the illusion that we can rely entirely on ourselves can shatter. This is when many people turn to God, realizing their own limitations. It offers only temporal solutions. Secular self-help can provide temporary relief by addressing the symptoms of a problem, such as an addiction or anxiety. However, a spiritual perspective teaches that sin is ultimately against God and requires a divine solution, not just a behavioral adjustment. It focuses on a temporary "fix." A solely humanistic approach is limited in that it cannot provide eternal solutions to spiritual problems.

It can Foster Selfishness

Paradoxically, a relentless focus on "self-improvement" can lead to increased self-centeredness and isolation. The self becomes the central focus. The self-help movement, in which the individual is the "sun in the center of it all," can inadvertently lead to selfishness. This inward focus can cause damage to relationships and undermine empathy. Healingmrequires a wider perspective.

In contrast, many spiritual traditions promote humility and service to others, which can help individuals overcome self-absorption. A healthy faith encourages turning outward and connecting with a community.

It Cannot Address Spiritual Brokenness

Trauma can create a spiritual wound that self-help cannot reach. A term known as pneumatraumatology describes trauma-related symptoms that impact a person's spiritual well-being, such as feelings of inadequacy and isolation. It ignores the need for supernatural help. Many who hold a spiritual worldview believe that some struggles require supernatural intervention, such as deliverance or inner healing. This is especially true for wounds believed to be exploited by demonic forces. It provides no ultimate meaning. When trauma shatters a person's worldview, self-help alone cannot provide a new, transcendent purpose. Faith can offer a way to find meaning in suffering by connecting with something larger than oneself.

The Spiritual Alternative

For those who embrace a faith-based approach, healing is not a solo journey. Instead, it is a collaborative effort with God, in which personal effort works in conjunction with divine grace.

The spiritual path to transformation includes:

- **Relying on God, not self:** In this view, self-reliance is not a virtue but a sin to be overcome. True transformation comes from God.

- **Finding truth in God's word:** The Bible is seen as a source of reliable truth that can free individuals from the lies and shame planted by trauma.

- **Seeking restoration in community:** Being part of a faith community provides accountability and encouragement, helping to counteract the isolation that trauma often creates.

- **Inviting God's presence:** Spiritual practices like prayer and inner healing are used to invite God's presence into painful memories, bringing peace and healing to a wounded soul.

Exposing lies: "You'll never change," "You're too damaged," "God doesn't love you"

To counter the lies "You'll never change," "You're too damaged," and "God doesn't love you," you must replace them with facts from psychology and faith. The following strategies challenge these cognitive distortions and build a stronger sense of self-worth.

Challenging The Lie: "You'll Never Change"

This is a cognitive distortion known as "all-or-nothing thinking" or "fortune-telling," which predicts a negative outcome without evidence.

Psychological Reframing.

1. Acknowledge that change takes time and effort. The first step is wanting to change, but lasting growth comes from developing self-awareness and practical coping skills.

2. Focus on small, consistent progress rather than expecting an overnight transformation.

3. Use the "catch it, check it, change it" technique. The next time the thought "I'll never change" arises, catch it, and then check it for accuracy.

4. Instead of saying, "I am always wrong," reframe it to, "I'm learning and growing".

5. Focus on your actions, not your identity. A negative action or mistake does not define your entire character. Remind yourself, "I made a mistake, but that doesn't make me a bad person".

Faith-Based Reframing

Embrace biblical promises of transformation. The Bible offers numerous examples of people who underwent significant change and scripture that speaks of spiritual renewal. *2 Corinthians 5:17 says, "Therefore, if anyone is in Christ, the new creation has come: The old has gone, the new is here!"* Exposing the lie: "You're too damaged." This is a false narrative that often comes from past experiences of betrayal, trauma, or emotional abuse.

Psychological Reframing

By focusing on God, Your worth is intrinsic. Self-worth is not dependent on your past failures, successes, or the opinions of others. You have inherent value, and no external event can take that away.

- Practice self-compassion. Instead of beating yourself up for perceived flaws, treat yourself with the same kindness and understanding you would offer a good friend.

- Acknowledging your struggles with kindness, rather than ignoring or judging your feelings, is the key to healing.

- Build a support network. Surround yourself with people who uplift and respect you. Toxic relationships can diminish your self-worth, while a positive support system can help validate your value.

- Faith-based reframing. You are a "masterpiece." *The Bible says you are "God's handiwork,"* a finished and intentional creation designed with care and love. Even in moments of feeling broken, your identity is not rooted in your damage but in your divine creation.

Challenging the lie: "God doesn't love you" This lie preys on feelings of isolation and despair, especially when life is difficult.

Psychological reframing: Accept your feelings without judgment. It's okay to feel abandoned or unloved. Acknowledge these emotions without letting them define your reality. Sometimes, our feelings can be fickle, and we need to use facts to ground ourselves. Focus on gratitude.

Shift your focus away from a perceived lack of love toward what is good in your life. Gratitude journaling can help build a more positive outlook.

Faith-based reframing: Remember the truth of the Cross. The cross is considered the ultimate proof of God's love. As *Romans 5:8* states, "But God demonstrates his own love for us in this: While we were still sinners, Christ died for us". Rely on scripture, not feelings. The lie that God doesn't love you comes from your "fickle feelings and thoughts," not from the unchangeable truth of Scripture. Read verses like *Romans 8:38–39*, which states nothing can separate you from God's love. The battle is spiritual. This destructive thought is often described as an attack from the enemy to steal your confidence and isolate you from God. Counteract this *ord rather than the chaos around you.*

Replacing lies with truth: God says, "You are chosen, healed, restored"

Based on Christian scripture, you can replace the lies about your worth and fate with the truth that God has chosen you, healed you, and restored you. This involves renewing your mind with specific biblical affirmations to counter the negative thoughts and self-perception. To address feelings of being overlooked or rejected, consider the biblical perspective that you are chosen. The Bible describes believers as a "chosen race, a royal priesthood, a holy nation, God's special possession". Scriptures like 1 Peter 2:9, Jeremiah 1:5, and John 15:16 highlight God's deliberate choice and purpose for individuals.

When dealing with feelings of brokenness or shame, the concept of being healed through faith is presented in scripture. This healing addresses spiritual, emotional, and physical hurts, offering peace and wholeness. Isaiah 53:5, Psalm 147:3, and Jeremiah 30:17 are among the verses that speak of God's ability to heal and restore. For those who feel beyond hope, the biblical message is one of restoration. It is believed that God can renew what was lost, bringing a new beginning and strength.

Scriptures such as 1 Peter 5:10, Joel 2:25, and Psalm 23:3 offer promises of restoration and renewed strength.

To actively replace negative thoughts with biblical truth, several steps are suggested:

1. Identify the false thought or lie.

2. Use specific Bible verses to counter the lie.

3. Speak the truth from scripture out loud.

4. Consistently repeat this process for ongoing mind renewal.

Treasured Child of God, You Will Not Stay Where Trauma Left You!

"You will not stay where trauma left you" signifies a declaration of healing and liberation. It is an affirmation that past pain does not have the final say and that a new future of restoration is possible. This message resonates with many who seek to move forward from emotional or psychological distress.

Interpretations From a Faith Perspective

A promise of divine order restoration. This phrase can be understood as a prophetic word declaring that God will not leave you in a state of brokenness. Instead, he promises to bring healing, redeem your pain for a greater purpose, and restore the years that were stolen by trauma. An invitation to move forward in healing. It is a call to partner with God in the healing process. While acknowledging that the trauma occurred, it denies that the event has the right to control your future. It encourages a move from a place of avoidance to one of intentional healing. Freedom from defining your identity by trauma. From a biblical worldview, your identity is not defined by the traumatic events you experienced. You are seen as a TREASURED child of God, not as a victim. This message encourages you to reject the "victim mentality" and embrace a new identity as a survivor, or even a victor.

Empowerment OVER Demonic Influence

In some spiritual traditions, unresolved trauma is viewed as an open door for demonic oppression. "Staying where trauma left you" is a declaration of deliverance, breaking the spiritual strongholds that may have formed around the pain.

Interpretations from a Psychological Perspective

Reframing the trauma narrative, works against common cognitive distortions that keep people trapped in the past. It offers a powerful reframe, moving the focus from the identity of a "damaged" person to one who is in the process of healing and growth. Embracing the possibility of change. The message directly counters the fatalistic thinking of "I'll never change" that often accompanies trauma. It instills hope by affirming that change is not only possible but destined.

This aligns with therapeutic approaches that emphasize agency and a forward-looking perspective. Encouraging action toward a new future, movement from a static, painful state to a dynamic, forward-moving one. Take actionable steps toward healing, such as seeking counseling, building supportive relationships, or engaging in other therapeutic practices.

"You will not stay where trauma left you" serves as a beacon of hope, reminding individuals that their past does not dictate their future. Be empowered to pursue healing and restoration, whether through faith, therapeutic practices, or both.

Chapter 4

GOD, THE ONLY TRUE RESTORER

"So I will restore to you the years that the swarming locust has eaten, the crawling locust, the consuming locust, And the chewing locust, My great army which I sent among you." Joel 2:25

Why Only The Trinity Can Heal The Depths of the Soul?

The Role of Each Person of The Trinity in Healing

God the Father: The source of love and belonging

Adoption into the family

The Father is seen as the ultimate source of unconditional love and acceptance. Trauma often creates deep feelings of rejection and abandonment. The doctrine of adoption teaches that, through Christ, believers are welcomed into God's family, healing the sense of being an outsider.

Intrinsic Worth and Identity

The Father's creative act gives every individual inherent value, countering the lie that a person is "too damaged" to be loved. This truth about one's intrinsic worth forms the stable foundation upon which deeper healing is built.

Sovereign Perspective

God the Father has a sovereign perspective over aØ of history, including our suffering. Trusting in His ultimate plan provides a sense of security and purpose, even when the causes of trauma are incomprehensible.

Testimonies from the Bible: Joseph, Job, David.

Testimonies from the Bible, such as those of Joseph, Job, and David, serve as powerful examples of how faith and the Trinitarian nature of God can be instrumental in healing from trauma. Each story illustrates a distinct aspect of trauma and its spiritual resolution through divine intervention and human perseverance.

- **Joseph**

Joseph experienced deep trauma at the hands of his own brothers, who were jealous of their father's favoritism toward him.

Trauma Endured: Betrayal, abuse, and human trafficking by his brothers. Wrongful imprisonment for years after being falsely accused of sexual assault.

God's Healing: God's presence remained with Joseph throughout his ordeal, providing favor even in slavery and prison. Joseph's faith in God's sovereign plan allowed him to reframe his trauma, seeing it not as an evil act by his brothers but as God's means to preserve his family during a famine.

Restoration achieved: Instead of seeking revenge, Joseph forgave his brothers and was restored to his family. This forgiveness broke the cycle of bitterness and allowed for the family's reconciliation and survival.

Relevance to Healing: Joseph's testimony demonstrates that healing is not about ignoring the pain but trusting that God can use even the most malicious acts for good. His forgiveness showcases how releasing the need for revenge can lead to peace and freedom.

- **Job**

Job was a righteous man who suffered immense loss and physical agony, yet his story illustrates that not all suffering is a punishment for sin.

Trauma Endured: The loss of his children, his wealth, and his health, followed by accusations from his friends that his suffering was due to a hidden sin.

God's Healing: God responded to Job not by explaining the cause of his suffering but by revealing His own infinite power and wisdom. Job's encounter with God moved him from demanding answers to resting in God's sovereignty.

Restoration Achieved: After humbling himself before God and praying for his accusers, Job was fully restored with twice the possessions and a new family.

Relevance to Healing: Job's story teaches that trusting in God's character is more important than understanding the reasons for our pain.

It provides hope that God can redeem what was lost and give strength during incomprehensible suffering.

- **David**

David, despite being a "man after God's own heart," committed grievous sins and experienced trauma from both others and his own poor choices.

Trauma Endured: David faced years of persecution from a jealous King Saul, but his most profound trauma came from his own actions: his adultery with Bathsheba and the murder of her husband, Uriah. The consequences of this sin led to familial trauma, including the rape of his daughter and his son Absalom's rebellion.

God's Healing: When confronted by the prophet Nathan, David showed authentic and heartfelt repentance, acknowledging his sin against God. In his Psalms (like Psalm 51), David repeatedly models how to cry out to God with honesty about his pain, fear, and guilt, placing his hope entirely in God's forgiveness and mercy.

Restoration Achieved: God forgave David, though he still had to endure the consequences of his actions. This process demonstrated that genuine repentance leads to spiritual restoration, even when earthly consequences remain.

Relevance to Healing: David's life shows that even great believers can make devastating mistakes and that sin can create its own trauma. However, his testimony offers a blueprint for repentance and how God provides mercy and restoration to those who honestly turn to Him.

In each of these testimonies, healing is not a human effort alone but a divine intervention powered by the Father's love, the Son's redemption, and the Spirit's comfort, resulting in a restoration that often surpasses the original state

The Process of Divine Order, Trinity Restores US in Stages

The restoration of a person is understood as a dynamic process guided by the Trinitarian nature of God: the Father orchestrates, the Son reconciles and redeems, and the Holy Spirit empowers and sanctifies. This process is not a single, instantaneous event, but a series of stages that reflect the divine order established for healing and transformation.

Stage 1: The Father Restores Divine Order and Identity

- The foundation of identity: As the origin of all creation, God the Father establishes the inherent worth and purpose of an individual. Trauma disrupts a person's sense of self and order, but the Father's restorative work begins by re-establishing a proper spiritual identity rooted in His unconditional love.

- Adoption and belonging: The ultimate source of acceptance, the Father, restores a person's sense of belonging by adopting them into His family through Jesus Christ. This counters the profound loneliness and rejection that often accompany deep wounds.

- Sovereign perspective: Trust in the Father's sovereign plan allows an individual to see that their trauma was not an accident but a part of a larger divine narrative, which brings a sense of peace and security.

Stage 2: The Son Brings Reconciliation and Redemption

ASPECT	REPAIR (HUMAN-CENTERED)	TRANSFORMATION (DIVINELY-LED)
Focus	Making things "almost as good as new" by patching up flaws.	Creating something entirely new and more beautiful than the original.
Effort	Relies on willpower and human effort to overcome past failures.	Requires surrender and trust in God's ability to create beauty from brokenness.

ASPECT	REPAIR (HUMAN-CENTERED)	TRANSFORMATION (DIVINELY-LED)
Outcome	Conceals cracks and imperfections to restore a facade of perfection.	Uses the scars and wounds to tell a story of redemption, making them a testament to God's grace.
Narrative	Holds onto the narrative of being "damaged" or "beyond repair".	Redeems the past by weaving it into a new, purposeful story of resilience

The Transformation Process

This prophetic insight points to a process that transcends human limitations and invites a divine perspective: Like beauty from ashes; The Bible promises that God can give a "crown of beauty instead of ashes" and "joy instead of mourning" (Isaiah 61:3).

This metaphor implies that the very material of our pain is used to create a new, beautiful work of grace. The art of Kintsugi in this concept is reflected in the Japanese art of Kintsugi, where broken pottery is repaired with lacquer mixed with gold dust.

- Empathy and suffering: As the incarnate Son, Jesus provides the ultimate empathy, having experienced human suffering firsthand. This connects with a person's pain, offering a compassionate presence that validates their experience.

- Redeeming the past Christ's sacrifice on the cross redeems the spiritual and emotional consequences of sin and trauma. This does not erase the past but breaks its power over an individual's life by bringing forgiveness and reconciliation with God. The past is not forgotten but is transformed from a source of shame into a testament of God's redemptive power.

- Healing the spiritual core Jesus provides the path to righteousness, addressing the spiritual core of the trauma and breaking the cycles of harmful coping mechanisms. This is the stage where the power of the past is surrendered to Christ.

Stage 3: The Holy Spirit Empowers and Renews

- Intimate presence The Holy Spirit acts as the Comforter, offering intimate and ongoing presence to soothe the pain of trauma. This personal companionship provides strength and guidance throughout the healing process.

- Mind and heart renewal Through the Spirit, the mind and heart are renewed, replacing trauma-based lies with biblical truth. This is a continuous process that retrains emotional responses and thought patterns corrupted by past hurt.

- Empowerment for a new life The Holy Spirit empowers individuals to break free from the past and live a transformed life. This is the stage of ongoing sanctification, where a person is equipped to be a "wounded healer" and walk in their new identity.

The Process of Divine Order in Healing

This staged process follows the "divine order," a purposeful and structured arrangement orchestrated by God. It moves from establishing the foundation of identity (the Father) to reconciling the trauma itself (the Son) to the ongoing work of transformation and empowerment (the Holy Spirit). The ultimate goal of this process is for an individual to reflect the life of the Trinity—a life of peace, love, and community.

Prophetic Insight: Restoration is Not Just Repair, It's Transformation.

Divine healing is a deeper, more profound process than simply fixing what is broken. While repair returns something to its original state, this insight promises a renewal that makes a person better, stronger, and more whole than they were before the trauma.

Key differences: Repair Vs. Transformation

Instead of hiding the cracks, the gold highlights them, celebrating the piece's history and making it more valuable and beautiful than it was originally. In a spiritual sense, the gold is the restoring grace of God, which makes us stronger and more radiant through our healing journey. Renewal of the mind is Transformation! Internal work of the Holy Spirit, which "renews" the mind to align with God's will (Romans 12:2).

This moves beyond just changing behavior to shifting one's entire perspective and core identity. Becoming a new creation is the ultimate goal of divine restoration is a spiritual transformation where we become a "new creation" in Christ (2 Corinthians 5:17). The old person gives way to a new identity shaped by grace, purpose, and renewal.

Ultimately, the insight that "restoration is not just repair" it is a prophetic encouragement to hold on to a higher hope—that God's work in a person's life goes beyond simple fixes, resulting in a glorious transformation.

Scripture anchor: "I will restore to you the years the locusts have eaten." (Joel 2:25).

Chapter 5

POWER OVER DARKNESS

Spiritual Warfare Explained Simply

Spiritual warfare is the unseen battle fought between the forces of God and the forces of evil (Satan and demons) for control over the human heart. It is an ongoing struggle that every believer is involved in, whether they realize it or not. This battle is not a physical conflict but a spiritual one, primarily fought in the mind through tactics like temptation, deception, and distraction.

The Battlefield: Your Mind

The devil and his forces primarily target your mind to undermine your faith and relationship with God. The tactics they use include: Creating doubt: Planting seeds of suspicion about God's goodness and promises. Feeding condemnation: Reminding you of your past sins to make you feel worthless and beyond forgiveness. Causing distraction: Pulling your focus toward worldly desires and away from spiritual growth. Fostering fear and despair: Exploiting your anxieties to make you feel helpless and overwhelmed. Promoting sin: Enticing you toward selfish, worldly, or immoral actions.

The "Armor of God": Your Defense

The Bible, particularly in Ephesians 6:10-18, outlines the spiritual armor believers can use to resist these attacks.

- Belt of truth: Holding fast to God's Word protects against Satan's lies and deceptions.

- Breastplate of righteousness: Living a righteous life, made possible through Jesus, guards your heart from sinful desires.

- Shield of faith: Actively trusting in God's promises can extinguish the fiery attacks of the enemy.

- Helmet of salvation: The assurance of your salvation protects your mind from doubt and despair.

- Sword of the Spirit (God's Word): Scripture is the one offensive weapon for dismantling the enemy's false arguments.

- Shoes of the Gospel of peace: Being prepared to share the good news keeps you grounded in your purpose.

The Battle Belongs to The Father, Son and Holy Spirit

While believers must participate in this fight, they are not meant to do it in their own strength.

Christ has already won: Jesus's death and resurrection defeated the devil, so believers fight from a position of victory, not desperation.

Victory is assured: As a child of God, no spiritual enemy can ultimately take your salvation away from you.

Rely on the Holy Spirit: The Holy Spirit empowers believers with divine strength and helps them in their prayers.

Stand firm: You overcome by resisting the enemy's schemes and submitting yourself to God, not by fighting spiritual forces directly.

Don't mistake every struggle for warfare: Not all hardships in life are demonic attacks. Some are simply the result of living in a fallen world or our decisions. Either way the Father, Son and the Holy Spirit.

My Experience as a Prophetess: Confronting Witches, Warlocks, and Demonic Powers

Acknowledging the Battle

Anyone engaged in spiritual warfare, recognizes that the conflict is not with people, but with spiritual forces of evil. This perspective prevents personal attacks and instead focuses on confronting the demonic powers influencing the situation. The enemy's tactics are identified, such as generating confusion, accusation, condemnation, and intimidation. A prophet, guided by the Holy Spirit, can discern these tactics and expose them, rendering them powerless in Jesus' name.

The Authority of Christ Jesus

Christ teaches us that confronting spiritual darkness is not done through one's own power but through the authority of Jesus Christ. The name of Jesus causes demons to tremble, and any power of witchcraft is considered ineffectual against a believer acting in Christ's authority. The prophetic voice declares Christ's supremacy and uses His authority to rebuke and cancel demonic assignments in Christ Jesus name!.

Offensive and Defensive Strategies

Offensive: The primary offensive weapon is the "Sword of the Spirit," which is the Word of God. Scripture is used to dismantle the enemy's lies and challenge demonic strongholds.

Defensive: The "Armor of God" (Ephesians 6:10-18) is put on through prayer and by living a righteous life rooted in faith, truth, and salvation. This armor protects the believer's heart and mind from demonic attacks.

Confronting Specific Manifestations

Witchcraft and curses: A prophetic voice confronts the spirit of witchcraft, which often operates through manipulation and control, similar to the biblical figure of Jezebel. The response is not to retaliate in the flesh but to break the curses through prayer and by blessing those involved.

Exposing hidden ploys: The prophetic anointing brings clarity and exposes hidden demonic agendas. This often involves revealing the motive behind negative actions, such as isolating prophetic people or promoting fear.

Breaking agreements: Confronting demonic influence can involve leading a person to repent and renounce past involvement with the occult, which breaks any legal right that demons have been given to access their life.

The Importance of Prayer and Humility

Continuous and strategic prayer is a crucial part of spiritual warfare. This can involve praying for protection, confessing Scripture, and binding demonic forces. Humility is essential, as spiritual strength comes from dependence on God, not personal power. Arrogance or pride can give the enemy an opportunity to attack.

Authority of the believer: Walking in the Power of Jesus' name.

The authority of the believer is the spiritual power and right to enforce Jesus' victory on Earth. This authority is not inherent to the person but is a delegated power derived from Christ, which is activated by faith and exercised in Jesus' name.

The Source of the Believer's Authority

Delegated by Christ: Before His ascension, Jesus declared, "All authority in heaven and on earth has been given to Me" (Matthew 28:18). He then delegated this authority to His followers to carry out His work, which includes making disciples and ministering in His name.

Positioned with Christ: The Bible states that believers have been "seated... in the heavenly realms with Christ Jesus" (Ephesians 2:6, NLT). This heavenly seating next to God places believers in a position of power and authority, with the devil and his forces beneath their feet.

Empowered by the Holy Spirit: Jesus promised His disciples that they would receive power when the Holy Spirit came upon them (Acts 1:8). This power enables believers to fulfill the mission of the Great Commission and wield the authority Jesus has given them.

How Believers Walk in This Authority

Walking in the power of Jesus' name is a conscious act of faith and obedience, not an automatic benefit.

Activating Faith: Knowledge of spiritual authority is not enough; it must be acted upon through faith. When faced with a spiritual challenge, believers can speak God's Word in faith, releasing the power of Jesus' name.

Exercising in Prayer: Believers can approach God with boldness and confidence, praying in Jesus' name to access His power. Jesus promised, "I will do whatever you ask in My name".

Ministering to Others: This authority is exercised in ministering to others, such as healing the sick and casting out demons. As demonstrated by Peter and John, the power is not in the believer, but in the name of Jesus.

Submitting to God: As James 4:7 instructs, "Submit yourselves, then, to God. Resist the devil, and he will flee from you." Submission to God is the foundation for effective resistance against evil forces.

Areas of Authority

The delegated authority of the believer is meant to be used actively in daily life to confront the schemes of the enemy.

Biblical examples of this authority include:

Healing the Sick: Jesus told believers that they would "lay hands on sick people, and they will get well" (Mark 16:18).

Casting Out Demons: Believers have the power to cast out demons in Jesus' name (Mark 16:17). The early church acted on this authority to drive out evil spirits.

Overcoming the Enemy: Jesus gave believers "authority to trample on snakes and scorpions and to overcome all the power of the enemy" (Luke 10:19).

Proclaiming the Gospel: As ambassadors for Christ, believers speak with His authority when they share His Word.

Prayer Strategies: Binding, Loosing, Covering your Mind and Home

The biblical concepts of binding, loosing, and covering are central to spiritual warfare in Christian prayer. They are based on the authority given to believers by Jesus Christ and involve active, faith-filled declarations.

The Strategy of Binding and Loosing

The strategy of binding and losing is based on Jesus' words in Matthew 18:18, where He gave His disciples authority. It is an act of exercising Christ's authority to restrict the enemy's activities and release God's will.

Binding

What It Is: A prayerful declaration that prevents or forbids spiritual forces from carrying out their will. It is a way of "tying up" the enemy's plans.

What To Bind: Evil spirits assigned to cause harm, confusion, or deception. Witchcraft and curses spoken against you or your family. Negative patterns of thinking, such as fear, depression, and anxiety.

How To Do It: Begin with praise and surrender to God, then specifically name what you are binding in Jesus' name.

Prophetic Prayer: *"In the name of Jesus, I bind every spirit of fear and anxiety in my life AND SEND IT BACK TO SENDER IN JESUS NAME!."*

Loosing

What It Is: A prayerful declaration that releases or permits what is in alignment with God's will and purpose. It is the counter-action to binding.

What To loose: The Holy Spirit's presence and gifts. Divine ORDER, peace, joy, healing, and prosperity. Spiritual breakthrough and forward momentum in your life.

How To Do It: After binding the negative force, declare the positive, biblical opposite.

Prophetic Prayer: *"I loose the peace of God over my mind and heart. I loose joy and spiritual freedom in my life IN CHRIST JESUS NAME."*

The Strategy of Covering with the Blood of Jesus

This prayer strategy focuses on the protective power of Christ's sacrifice on the cross. It is an act of faith that applies the spiritual covering of Jesus' blood over a person, place, or situation.

Covering Your Mind

The mind is a primary battlefield for spiritual attacks, with the enemy often planting lies, doubts, and negative thoughts.

Strategy: Daily pray to cover your mind and thoughts with the blood of Jesus. This protects your thought life and helps take every thought "captive to the obedience of Christ" (2 Corinthians 10:5).

Example Prayer: *"I cover my mind with the blood of Jesus. I declare that I have the mind of Christ and that every deceptive and intrusive thought must be silent IN CHRIST JESUS NAME."*

Covering Your Home

Dedicating your home to God and covering it with prayer is a strategy for creating a sanctuary from evil influence.

Strategy

- **Remove Ungodly Items:** Before or during the prayer, remove any items that could give spiritual evil a "foothold," such as media or objects related to the occult.

- **Declare God's Ownership:** Walk through each room of your home, verbally dedicating it to God's purpose and presence.

- **Cover With Blood of Jesus:** Anoint each doorpost and window with holy oil, holy water salt dedicated to the Father, Son and the Holy-Spirit is (a covenant act) while pleading the blood of Jesus over the entrance.

Prophetic Prayer: *"I dedicate this home to you, Lord Jesus. I cover every room with Your precious blood and declare that this home is a place of peace, sanctuary, and Your Holy Spirit. I cancel every curse and break every evil assignment against this house in Jesus' name."*

Scripture Anchor: *"For the weapons of our warfare are not carnal, but mighty through God to the pulling down of strongholds." (2 Corinthians 10:4).*

Chapter 6

THE PATH OF HEALING THROUGH THE FATHER, THE SON AND THE HOLY SPIRIT

By the Father's deep and merciful love, you are known and seen. Through the finished work of the Son, Jesus Christ, you are declared whole and redeemed. And by the intimate, transformative presence of the Holy Spirit, the life-giving power of God is made active within you, bringing comfort, restoration, and peace to your spirit, soul, and body.

Practical Steps to Healing

Healing is a holistic journey that involves practical steps for the mind, body, and spirit. The process is not linear and requires patience and self-compassion.

- **Acknowledge and Process Feelings:** Allow yourself to feel sadness, anger, and grief without judgment. Journaling can be a powerful tool for expressing and understanding complex emotions.

- **Practice Forgiveness:** This involves letting go of resentment toward others and yourself. It does not mean excusing hurtful behavior, but rather releasing its power over you.

- **Set Healthy Boundaries:** Learn to say "no" to requests or limit contact with individuals who drain your energy or are toxic. This protects your emotional well-being and prevents further harm.

- **Work With a Therapist:** For deep trauma or mental health conditions, a professional can provide guided support. Therapies like Cognitive Behavioral Therapy (CBT) or Eye Movement Desensitization and Reprocessing (EMDR) are specifically designed for trauma recovery.

- **Embrace Mindfulness:** Techniques such as deep breathing, meditation, and grounding can anchor you in the present, reducing stress and anxiety.

- **Challenge Negative Thoughts:** Identify and reframe unhelpful thought patterns. Instead of dwelling on past failures, look for opportunities for growth.

For the Body and Physical Health

Prioritize Self-Care: Regularly engage in activities that bring you joy and help you relax, such as hobbies, reading, or spending time in nature.

Engage in Regular Movement: Exercise, from gentle walks to yoga, can boost your mood and help release pent-up emotional energy.

Nourish Yourself: Focus on eating healthy, balanced meals and staying hydrated. Proper nutrition is critical for both mental and physical recovery.

Improve Sleep Hygiene: Aim for 7 to 9 hours of quality sleep per night. Sleep is essential for the body's natural processes of physical and emotional repair.

For the Spirit and Connection

Practice Gratitude: Shifting your focus to what you are thankful for, even small things, can increase your sense of well-being. Keeping a gratitude journal can make this a daily practice.

Seek Supportive Community: Build a network of trusted friends, family, or a faith-based group who can offer encouragement without judgment.

Connect with Nature: Spending time outdoors can be deeply grounding and help restore a sense of calm and perspective.

Engage in Spiritual Practices: Activities like prayer, meditation, or quiet reflection can help you feel more connected to a deeper purpose or a higher power.

Serve Others: Volunteering or engaging in acts of kindness can shift your focus away from your pain and towards a greater purpose.

Prayer and Intimacy with God

Prayer is a primary way to cultivate intimacy with God, moving beyond mere religious duty to a deep, personal relationship. It is about communicating with God, learning to listen, and experiencing his presence in your daily life.

Cultivating Intimacy Through Prayer

- Just as with any meaningful relationship, an intimate connection with God requires intentional time.

- Set aside a consistent time and place. Jesus often withdrew to quiet, solitary places to pray to his Father (1. Prioritize a dedicated timeLuke 5:16). This models the importance of separating yourself from distractions.

- Start with a small commitment. If a long, uninterrupted session seems daunting, start with 10–15 minutes and grow from there. The consistency is more important than the length.

Broaden your Definition of Prayer

Prayer is more than a list of requests. Expanding your view of prayer can deepen your intimacy with God.

Use the A.C.T.S. model: This structure can help guide your prayers beyond requests.

- **Adoration:** Start by praising God for who he is—his goodness, power, and mercy.

- **Confession:** Humbly acknowledge your faults and repent. This removes barriers and prepares your heart to receive from God.

- **Thanksgiving:** Thank God for his abundant blessings, both big and small. A grateful heart draws you closer to him.

- **Supplication:** Bring your needs and the needs of others to him. This is an act of dependence on God.

Talk to God like a Friend

You don't need eloquent or "flowery" language to speak to God.

- Be honest and open. Tell him about your frustrations, fears, and hopes. He already knows your heart, but expressing it builds trust and intimacy.

- Involve him throughout your day. Don't limit your conversation with God to a dedicated prayer time. Talk to him while driving, cooking, or walking. Acknowledge his presence in everything you do.

Practice Listening

Intimacy is a two-way street. Prayer is not just about talking; it is also about listening.

- Incorporate silence. After you have spoken, sit in quiet expectation. Rest in his presence without striving to hear a specific message.

- Ask God to reveal himself through Scripture. As you read the Bible, ask the Holy Spirit to speak to you and reveal something new about God's nature. This makes reading a conversation, not just a study.

Integrate Worship and Scripture

Worship and Bible reading are powerful forms of prayer that enhance intimacy.

- Worship: Play worship music that glorifies God and praise him in song. This shifts your focus from your needs to his greatness and presence.

- Pray the Scriptures: Praying using verses from the Bible aligns your heart and words with God's will. For example, pray John 17:26, asking that the love the Father has for Jesus may be in you.

Remove Common Barriers

Sometimes, intimacy with God is hindered by things that get in the way.

- Address busyness. If you are too busy for God, you are too busy. Make your prayer time a major, non-negotiable priority.

- Deal with pride and shame. Pride convinces you that you don't need God, and shame convinces you that you are unworthy of him. Be quick to repent and remember that he is eager to forgive and embrace you.

Forgiveness (Even When it feels Impossible)

Forgiveness is an intentional, often challenging, process of releasing resentment and anger, especially when it feels impossible. It is not about condoning the offense or pretending it didn't hurt; it is about freeing yourself from the bitterness that chains you to the past

Forgiveness can be broken down into practical steps for both psychological and spiritual well-being.

Psychological Steps to Release Resentment

- Acknowledge and accept your pain. The first step is to validate your feelings of hurt and anger instead of suppressing them. Acknowledging the depth of your pain is necessary for beginning the healing process.

- Understand that forgiveness is a gift to yourself. Holding a grudge only harms you by allowing the person who wronged you to continue having power over your emotions. Forgiveness is an act of self-care and a choice to move forward.

- Decide to forgive. Forgiveness is a conscious decision, not a feeling. You may not feel like forgiving, but you can choose to release the offender from the debt they owe you.

- Release the need for revenge. You can entrust the concept of justice to a higher power or legal system, but let go of your personal desire to seek retaliation.

- Reframe the narrative. Try to find meaning in your pain by reflecting on how you have grown from the experience. Did you develop more empathy, resilience, or stronger boundaries?

- Set healthy boundaries (Forgive, but don't forget). Forgiveness does not mean forgetting the offense. You can forgive someone without placing yourself in a situation where they can harm you again. This is especially important if the person is unrepentant. Forgiveness does not automatically require reconciliation.

Spiritual Steps to Lean on God's Grace

- Confess your unforgiveness to God. Honestly tell God that you are struggling and that you don't have the strength to forgive on your own. King David modeled this kind of raw honesty in the Psalms.

- Remember the forgiveness you have received. Reflect on the immense debt that God forgave you through Christ. This can provide perspective and motivation to extend that same grace to others.

- Pray for the person who hurt you. Jesus commanded us to "pray for those who persecute you" (Matthew 5:44). While this may feel impossible, praying for blessings for your offender can soften your heart over time.

- Trust that God will handle it. Give your pain to God and trust that vengeance belongs to Him alone (Romans 12:19). This releases the burden from your shoulders and places it in God's capable hands.

- Repeat as necessary. When painful memories resurface, remind yourself and God of your decision to forgive. The process is a journey, and you may need to choose to forgive repeatedly until the pain eventually loses its grip.

Counseling and Wise Mentorship

Counseling and wise mentorship are distinct yet complementary avenues for guidance, both rooted in the principle that no one is meant to walk their path alone. While counseling often addresses and heals past hurts, mentorship is typically a more forward-looking relationship focused on growth and development.

Counseling: Professional Healing and Guidance

Counseling is a formal, problem-focused relationship with a trained professional, such as a licensed therapist or a pastoral counselor. It is often intended to be a shorter-term relationship focused on a specific mental health issue or life struggle.

Key Benefits of Counseling

- **Healing From Past Trauma:** A trained therapist can help you explore and process past hurts, identifying how they may be impacting your present life and equipping you with coping skills.

- **Improved Emotional Regulation:** Counseling can teach you how to better manage and express your emotions, including anger, anxiety, and depression.

- **A Safe, Confidential Space:** It provides a judgment-free environment to talk through problems and navigate difficult life changes.

- **Identifying Negative Patterns:** It helps you become more aware of self-defeating behaviors and thought processes, allowing you to change them.

- **Spiritual Integration (Pastoral Counseling):** A pastoral counselor combines clinical methods with spiritual care, helping you explore how your faith and values affect your struggles.

Wise Mentorship: A Relationship for Growth

Mentorship is an informal, long-term relationship with a trusted person who has experience and character you admire. This relationship is focused on holistic development, helping you grow in character, wisdom, and skills for the future.

Key Characteristics of a Wise Mentor

- **Offers Future-Focused Wisdom:** A wise mentor can provide guidance and help you navigate your path because they have walked a similar one before.

- **Serves as a Role Model:** A mentor provides guidance through both their advice and their example, modeling godly character and healthy habits.

- **Provides Honest Accountability:** A wise mentor is committed to your growth and will be honest with you, calling you to return to a path of integrity when you stray.

- **Offers Unbiased Advice:** Though personal, the mentorship is not so emotionally close that the mentor cannot offer honest and objective feedback.

- **Promotes Mutual Growth:** The mentor-mentee relationship should not be one-sided. A wise mentor also benefits from the relationship, experiencing personal and spiritual growth alongside their mentee.

Integrating Counseling and Wise Mentorship

The two approaches are not mutually exclusive and can work in tandem.

Use Counseling to Address Deeper Issues: If you have past trauma or persistent mental health struggles, professional counseling can provide the focused, intensive healing needed before moving forward.

Use a Mentor for Forward Guidance: Once you have worked through past hurts in counseling, a mentor can help you apply that healing and grow into the person you are becoming.

Allow For a Clear Referral: A wise mentor should know their boundaries. If your conversation with a mentor veers into issues requiring professional treatment, they should refer you to a trained counselor.

The Biblical Perspective

The Bible consistently advocates for seeking wise counsel, and the Book of Proverbs is filled with verses on the topic.

The Danger of Ignoring Counsel: "The way of a fool is right in his own eyes, but a wise man listens to advice" (Proverbs 12:15, ESV).

Safety in Many Counselors: "Where there is no guidance, a people falls, but in an abundance of counselors there is safety" (Proverbs 11:14, ESV).

The need for both: In a Christian context, counseling can be seen as receiving expert guidance to address specific problems, while mentorship is a more relational form of discipleship for life-on-life growth.

Foundational Biblical Principles

Transformation From the Inside Out: The concept is an inner renovation, not just a change in behavior. The mind, or heart, is the source of our attitudes and actions, and renewing it is crucial for spiritual growth.

Biblical Perspective Over Worldly Perspective: Paul contrasts being "conformed to this world" with being "transformed by the renewing of your mind". This means actively replacing cultural ways of thinking with God's perspective.

The Battle for Your Mind: Scripture describes the mind as a spiritual battlefield, where we must take every thought captive and make it obedient to Christ, replacing lies with God's truth.

Practical Steps for Daily Renewal

- **Immerse Yourself in Scripture:** God's Word is the primary tool for transformation. Read, meditate on, and memorize scripture daily to allow the Holy Spirit to reshape your thinking.

- **Identify and Replace Lies With Truth:** Pay attention to negative or worldly thoughts that arise, such as "I'm not good enough" or "God won't forgive me." Actively replace these falsehoods with specific biblical truths, like "I am fearfully and wonderfully made" (Psalm 139:14).

- **Guard Your Inputs:** What you see, read, and listen to shapes your mind. Set boundaries around social media, news, and other entertainment to choose content that is "true, noble, right, pure, lovely, [and] admirable" (Philippians 4:8).

- **Engage in Consistent Prayer:** Use prayer to submit your thoughts to God and listen for His guidance. When you bring your anxieties to the Lord, He offers peace and perspective.

- **Speak Life Over Yourself:** Confess God's truth out loud, declaring your identity in Christ. This practice can actively reframe your mindset and build your faith.

- **Practice Gratitude:** Cultivating a grateful heart shifts your focus from what is lacking to the abundance of God's blessings in your life, leading to greater peace and joy.

- **Find Community:** Connect with other believers who can offer support, truth, and accountability. Surrounding yourself with people who speak life into you makes the renewal process more sustainable.

The Benefits of a Renewed Mind

Making a daily commitment to renewing your mind leads to profound changes in your life, including:

- **Greater Peace:** Aligning your thoughts with God's truth helps you experience a "peace that surpasses all understanding" - (Philippians 4:7).

- **Clarity and Discernment:** A renewed mind allows you to "test and approve what God's will is," leading to better decision-making.

- **Overcoming Negative Habits:** It empowers you to break free from negative emotional and thought patterns like worry, insecurity, and frustration.

- **Deeper Spiritual Growth:** This daily practice strengthens your relationship with God as you trust more fully in His guidance and grace.

Exercises: Journaling, Prayer Declarations, Scripture Meditation

Journaling, prayer declarations, and scripture meditation are complementary practices for Christians seeking to renew their minds and deepen their faith. Used together, they create a powerful system for internalizing biblical truth and aligning your thoughts and actions with God's will.

Journaling Exercises

Journaling is a form of reflective writing that allows you to process your thoughts and emotions, identify harmful mental patterns, and organize your prayers. It serves as a personal record of your spiritual journey, helping you track your growth over time.

Exercises:

Gratitude Journal: Begin by listing things you are grateful for, both big and small. Focusing on God's blessings cultivates a positive mindset and shifts your perspective away from worries or negativity.

Identify Lies and Replace With truth: Write down a persistent negative thought or lie you believe about yourself (e.g., "I am not good enough"). Below it, write the biblical truth that contradicts it (e.g., "I am fearfully and wonderfully made" based on Psalm 139:14).

Prayer Reflection: Use your journal to write out your prayers, confessing struggles and documenting God's answers. This practice helps you see God's faithfulness and makes your prayer life more intentional.

Spiritual Check-In: Answer self-reflection questions like:

- *What is my relationship with God like right now?*
- *What is one area where I need to grow in my faith?*
- *Where do I need to establish healthier boundaries in my life?*

Prayer Declarations

Prayer declarations are faith-filled statements based on God's promises in Scripture. This practice involves speaking God's Word over your circumstances to build faith and counteract doubt, fear, and negativity.

Exercises:

Personalize Scripture: Take a relevant Bible verse and personalize it by inserting your name or using "I" statements. For example, turn 2 Timothy 1:7 into, "I have been given a spirit of power, and of love, and of a sound mind".

Declare Identity In Christ: Speak statements out loud that affirm your new identity.

"I am a child of God, deeply loved and chosen."

"The same power that raised Christ from the dead lives in me".

Speak Over Circumstances: Declare breakthrough over specific areas of your life, such as your finances, health, or relationships.

"I declare freedom from the spirit of anxiety and fear".

"I declare open doors and divine favor in my career".

Use the Psalms: Pray passages from the Psalms, which are rich with expressions of both hardship and faith. For example, turn Psalm 91 into a personal declaration of God's protection.

Scripture Meditation

Biblical meditation is the practice of deeply thinking about and reflecting on God's Word. Unlike Eastern meditation, the goal is not to empty your mind but to fill it with Scripture.

Exercises:

- **Lectio Divina (Divine Reading):** This classic method involves four steps:

1. **Read:** Read a short passage of Scripture slowly and attentively.
2. **Reflect:** Chew on the words. What word or phrase stands out to you?
3. **Respond:** Talk to God about the passage. How does it apply to your life?

4. **Rest:** Sit silently in God's presence, allowing the words to sink into your heart.

- **Memorize and Repeat:** Choose a key verse to memorize. Repeat it to yourself throughout the day to keep your mind focused on God's truth, especially when negative thoughts arise.

- **Imagine the Scene:** If you are reading a story or account, try to visualize the scene in your mind. Place yourself in the story to understand it on a deeper level.

- **Mind Mapping:** Write a central Scripture in the middle of a page and draw lines to connect thoughts, ideas, and related verses that come to mind. This helps you explore the passage more fully.

By combining these three exercises, you can create a daily rhythm for spiritual growth that transforms your thoughts and strengthens your faith.

Scripture anchor: *"Be transformed by the renewing of your mind." (Romans 12:2).*

Chapter 7

BECOMING YOUR BEST SELF IN CHRIST

Moving Beyond Survival into Thriving

The journey from merely surviving to truly thriving is a transformation from a state of constant stress and anxiety to one of purpose, peace, and growth. This shift moves a person from being reactive and fearful to living intentionally and confidently.

What Surviving Looks Like

Survival mode is a constant state of hypervigilance, characterized by:

- **A reactive Mindset:** Decisions are driven by immediate threats and external circumstances, not intentional purpose.

- **Exhaustion and Overwhelm:** The body and mind are in a constant "fight, flight, or freeze" state, leading to burnout.

- **Feeling Stuck or Unfulfilled:** There is a heavy emotional burden of just getting through the day with little joy or connection.

- **Isolation and Comparison:** Social interactions feel draining, and it is easy to fall into comparing your struggles with the "highlight reels" of others.

What Thriving Looks Like

Thriving is a mindset of abundance, resilience, and joy, defined by:

- **Intentionality:** You are in control of your reactions and actively engage with life in alignment with your values.

- **Emotional Resilience:** You can experience a range of emotions without being overwhelmed and recover from setbacks with greater ease.

- **Purpose and Fulfillment:** You are engaged in activities that bring you joy and that align with your purpose.

- **Meaningful Connection:** Relationships are a source of strength and support, not obligation.

A Blueprint for Moving from Surviving to Thriving

The journey toward thriving is not about avoiding hard times but about growing through them. Here is a path to get there:

Acknowledge and Accept your Current Reality

1. **Notice and Reframe Your Thoughts:** Consciously recognize when you are operating in survival mode. Catch negative thought patterns and practice reframing them to a positive or neutral perspective.

2. **Embrace Your Emotions:** It's okay to not be okay. Acknowledge your struggles, talk to trusted friends, or seek professional counseling to process your emotions rather than suppressing them.

Reset your Nervous System and Regulate your Body

1. **Prioritize Rest and Self-Care:** Consistent, quality sleep, nourishing food, and proper hydration are not luxuries but necessities for moving beyond survival mode.

2. **Practice Mindfulness and Breathing:** When you feel overwhelmed, slow your pace and take deep, slow breaths. Mindfulness helps to stay present and regulate your body's stress response.

3. **Move Your Body:** Regular physical activity, even in small increments, boosts energy and mental well-being.

Cultivate Growth and Purpose

1. **Remember God's Past Faithfulness:** Recall and document times when God has helped you through difficult situations. This builds trust that he will help you again.

2. **Seek Godly Counsel:** As with all growth, wise, godly counsel from a mentor or spiritual director can provide new perspectives and guidance.

3. **Set Small, Meaningful Goals:** Focus on one small, intentional step you can take today. Celebrate these small wins to build momentum and reinforce positive habits.

4. **Discover Your "Why":** Reconnect with your passions and purpose. When you know your mission, the "how" becomes clear, and you can focus on activities that bring joy and fulfillment.

Embrace Community

1. **Strengthen Your Connections:** Prioritize spending time with friends, family, and church members who share your values. Social connection is vital for well-being.

2. **Set Healthy Boundaries:** Learn to say "no" to protect your time and energy. This is essential for maintaining your well-being and fostering positive relationships.

The journey from surviving to thriving is a process, not a destination. By taking small, intentional steps, you can move toward a more fulfilling and joyful life.

Discovering Identity in Christ: Loved, Chosen, Redeemed

Discovering and embracing their identity in Christ as loved, chosen, and redeemed is foundational to moving beyond a life of survival into one of thriving. This spiritual reality offers a new, unshakable foundation for self-worth, purpose, and peace, independent of worldly standards or past mistakes.

Loved: A Boundless and Unconditional Love

Understanding God's profound, unconditional love is the starting point for a secure identity.

Key truths:

- **His Love is Not Earned:** God's love is based on his character, not your performance or achievements. Romans 5:8 says, "But God shows his love for us in that while we were still sinners, Christ died for us".

- **You are Accepted:** You are not just tolerated but fully accepted and wanted. John 3:16 reminds believers of the immense sacrifice made out of love.

- **There is No Distance:** Nothing can separate you from God's love.

Romans 8:38–39 declares, "For I am sure that neither death nor life, nor angels nor rulers, nor things present nor things to come, nor powers, nor height nor depth, nor anything else in all creation, will be able to separate us from the love of God in Christ Jesus our Lord".

Chosen: Called with Purpose and Intention

Being chosen by God means you are part of his divine plan and purpose, not an accident or afterthought.

Key truths:

- **A Pre-Ordained Plan:** God had you in mind before the world began, predestining you for adoption through Jesus Christ. You can find more about this in Ephesians 1:4-5.

- **Part of a Special People:** You are called out of darkness into his marvelous light, belonging to a "chosen people, a royal priesthood, a holy nation, God's special possession".

- **Sealed By the Spirit:** The Holy Spirit serves as God's guarantee of your belonging and eternal inheritance.

Redeemed: Freed from the Past and Made New

Redemption signifies being bought back and set free from the power of sin to live a new life.

Key Truths:

- **A New Creation:** In Christ, you are a new person, no longer defined by past mistakes. 2 Corinthians 5:17 describes this transformation.

- **Forgiven and Cleansed:** Christ's blood paid the price for your freedom and complete forgiveness. Psalm 103:12 speaks of the removal of transgressions.

- **Empowered for New Life:** This new identity releases you from shame and guilt, enabling you to live in freedom and grace.

How To Live in Your Identity

Embracing this identity involves a daily process of spiritual renewal, replacing falsehoods with God's truth.

1. **Immerse Yourself in Scripture:** Meditate on verses about your identity in Christ, such as those in Ephesians 1-3.

2. **Repent and Confess:** Acknowledge believing lies and confess any sin hindering your relationship with God.

3. **Surround Yourself With Truth-Speakers:** Connect with other believers who can affirm your identity and help you overcome challenges.

4. **Live From Your Identity, Not For It:** Stop striving for acceptance and approval through performance; instead, live confidently based on the truth that you are already loved, chosen, and redeemed.

Purpose After Pain: Turning Testimony Into Ministry

Turning personal pain into ministry involves recognizing that God works through suffering to bring about purpose, not just for the individual, but for the good of others. A testimony of hardship, viewed through a biblical lens, becomes a powerful tool for compassion, empathy, and service.

The Theological Foundation

This process is rooted in a Christian understanding of suffering

Suffering is Not Pointless: Scripture does not glorify pain, but it shows how a sovereign God can redeem it. The pain that once defined your life can be used to forge your character, deepen your faith, and prepare you for your assignment.

A Weapon of Strength: As you surrender your wounds to God, he can transform them into "weapons of strength". Your experiences can become a source of profound wisdom and resilience.

Following the Example of Christ: Jesus, a "man of sorrows acquainted with grief," is the ultimate example of suffering for a greater purpose. His own suffering enables him to be our compassionate High Priest, understanding what we go through.

The Practical Journey from Pain to Purpose

This transition is not immediate but is a deliberate process of healing and refocusing

- **Process Your Pain With God**

1. **Acknowledge and Surrender:** Confess your pain and loss to God, and surrender your wounds to him. Do not ignore or numb your pain, but let it lead you into a deeper reliance on God, who "raises the dead".

2. **Wait and Trust:** Recognize that turning pain into purpose is a journey, and God's timing is perfect. Some of the most valuable lessons are learned in seasons of waiting.

3. **Reframe Your Narrative:** Begin to see your suffering not as the end of your story but as a pivotal part of it. Your testimony is not just about what you went through, but about how God brought you through it.

- **Cultivate Compassion and Empathy**

1. **Share Your Story for God's Glory:** Focus on what God has done, not on your struggles alone. An authentic testimony highlights how Christ has changed your life, making your story a relatable bridge for others.

2. **Connect Through Shared Humanity:** Your story allows others to realize they are not alone. Vulnerability becomes a source of strength that fosters deep connection and community.

3. **Move Beyond Empathy to Compassion:** Empathy is feeling another's pain. Compassion is being so moved by it that you are compelled to act. The experience of your own pain deepens your capacity for compassion toward others.

- **Serve and Use Your Testimony as Ministry**

1. **Seek Godly Counsel**: As you embark on ministry, seek wise counsel from mentors or pastors who can guide you with biblical wisdom and help you avoid common pitfalls.

2. **Start Small and Organically:** You do not need to create a formal ministry overnight. Start by reaching out to people you know, and allow God to grow it. Examples include:

   - Volunteering for a cause related to your experience.

   - Starting a small group to discuss your experience.

- Mentoring someone one-on-one.

3. **Center Christ in Your Ministry:** Your story is the illustration, but the Gospel is the message. A ministry that lasts must be centered on Christ and his transformative power, not on your personal history.

Building Confidence and Resilience Through Faith

Anchoring your self-worth and strength in your relationship with God, rather than relying on circumstances, achievements, or human validation. This spiritual foundation enables a person to face challenges and recover from setbacks with a perspective rooted in hope and a sense of purpose.

The Spiritual Foundation

- **Identity in Christ:** Confidence built on faith begins with an understanding of who you are in Christ—loved, chosen, and redeemed. This identity is a gift, not something to be earned, which means it cannot be lost.

- **Hope in God's Promises:** Resilience is sustained by hope, the long-term perspective that God is in control and has a good plan for your life. This hope acts as an anchor in the midst of life's storms.

- **God's Power in Weakness:** Instead of seeing weakness as a barrier, faith teaches that it is an opportunity for God's strength to be made perfect. Acknowledging your limitations allows you to draw on His power, giving you courage beyond your own ability.

Practical Steps for Building Confidence and Resilience

Cultivate an Inner Life Rooted in Truth

- **Renew Your Mind With Scripture:** Actively replace negative, fearful, or worldly thoughts with biblical truth through regular reading, meditation, and memorization.

Verses to reflect on: Philippians 4:13 ("I can do aØ things through Christ who strengthens me") and Isaiah 41:10 ("Do not fear, for I am with you") are excellent starting points.

- **Pray With Honesty and Trust:** Use prayer to communicate openly with God about your struggles and fears, but also to surrender control and express gratitude for what you have. This deepens your trust and cultivates peace.

Develop Positive and Healthy Habits

- **Practice Self-Discipline:** Small, consistent actions of obedience to God's will build confidence in your ability to follow His leading.

- **Practice Gratitude:** Journaling and giving thanks for God's blessings, even in difficult circumstances, shifts your focus from what is lacking to what is present. This is a crucial skill for overcoming anxiety.

- **Embrace Mistakes as Growth:** Understand that mistakes are not fatal to your faith. As a Christian, you will "fall" but will rise again because God upholds you.

Build a Support System

- **Connect With a Faith Community:** God designed us to live in a community, where we can encourage, support, and be accountable to one another.

- **Seek Godly Counsel:** When facing difficult seasons, seek wisdom from mature Christians, mentors, or counselors.

See Challenges as Opportunities

- **Find Purpose in Adversity:** Resilient Christians learn to reframe adversity not as pointless pain, but as a refining process orchestrated by God. Like Joseph, they trust that God is working all things for good, allowing them to turn a painful testimony into a powerful ministry.

- **Take Action in Faith:** Confidence grows when you act on your faith, stepping out in obedience even when you feel ill-equipped. This is where you witness God's power at work in your life.

Prophetic Reminder: "Your Best Self Is Your God-Self."

"Your best self is your God-self" means aligning your life with your identity in Christ, not a worldly image. It is not a call to become God, but to recognize that the truest and most authentic version of yourself is the one shaped by God's love and purpose.

What It Means

The Pursuit of God: Your best self is found not by seeking self-improvement alone, but by seeking God. It's a journey of surrendering your own will to become more like Jesus.

A New Foundation: This identity is based on God's unwavering love, not your performance or achievements. This provides a secure foundation for confidence and resilience.

Embracing God's Image: You were created in God's image, and your "God-self" is the original, good design he intended for you. It's about letting God restore and renew you into that original design.

A Contrast to Self-Worship: The statement challenges the idea that your best self is achieved through your own effort. Instead, it roots your worth and purpose in something eternal

Chapter 8

HELPING OTHERS HEAL

"Healing is not just for you—it's so you can help others," is deeply rooted in Christian teaching. The Bible explains that God comforts believers during trials so they, in turn, can comfort others with the same comfort they received from Him. This process transforms personal pain into purposeful ministry.

From Patient to Physician

As you heal, you transition from being the "patient needing help" to becoming the "physician" who offers it. This does not mean you have to become a licensed professional, but that your own experiences have uniquely equipped you to help others walking a similar path.

- **You Can Offer Empathy and Understanding:** If you have recovered from a severe illness, divorce, or childhood trauma, you know the pain, discouragement, and mental battles firsthand.

- **Your Perspective is Different:** You can confidently say, "I've been there, and I know you can make it through this." This is a powerful comfort that someone who hasn't experienced that specific struggle cannot offer in the same way.

Healing Qualifies You as a "Wounded Healer"

Theologian Henri Nouwen coined the term "wounded healer" to describe those who can minister out of their very place of pain.

1. **It Creates Compassion:** As you recognize your own brokenness and need for grace, you become more understanding of the struggles of others.

2. **It Offers Hope Through Testimony:** Your testimony is not just about what you went through, but about how God brought you through it. Sharing this with others gives them hope that God can and will do the same for them.

3. **It Leads to Intentional Service:** A healed person often moves from being internally focused to externally focused, seeking opportunities to share their story and assist others. This can be as simple as reaching out to someone with a listening ear or volunteering for a cause related to your experience.

Your Story Becomes a Tool for God's Glory

Instead of being a source of shame, your pain becomes a powerful illustration of God's grace and redemptive power. It is an opportunity to show that in the midst of circumstances that should have made you bitter or miserable, you found joy and hope in Christ.

Sharing Your Testimony as a Weapon

A testimony becomes a weapon when you share your story of how God brought you through a struggle. Your vulnerable and honest witness reveals God's power, shames the enemy, and brings hope to those facing similar battles. This is rooted in Revelation 12:11, where believers overcome Satan "by the blood of the Lamb and by the word of their testimony".

How to Share Your Testimony as a Weapon

To keep your testimony short and sweet, use this three-part structure:

- **Before:** Briefly describe what your life was like before Christ, focusing on a specific struggle or mindset. Keep it relatable and avoid excessive details.

- **How:** Explain the turning point when you encountered Jesus. Did a friend share the gospel with you? Did you face a difficult moment that led you to Him? This is the central, Christ-focused part of your story.

- **After:** Share how your life has changed since that encounter. Be honest that things aren't perfect, but emphasize the peace, purpose, and strength you have in Christ. This contrast shows the power of God's redemption.

The Purpose of Sharing

Your testimony is not for your own glory but for God's. Your Testimony:

- **Encourages Others:** Your story shows others that God is active and faithful, inspiring them to trust Him with their own struggles.

- **Exposes the Enemy:** By speaking openly about God's victory in your life, you silence the "accuser of the brethren" (Satan) and declare his defeat.

- **Declares the Gospel:** It provides a real-life illustration of the Gospel's transforming power, inviting others to experience the same hope.

How to Minister to Others Still Stuck in Trauma

Ministering to someone with unresolved trauma requires patience, compassion, and a careful approach that prioritizes their safety and healing process. Instead of trying to provide quick solutions, your role is to be a safe, non-judgmental presence who points them toward God's truth and when necessary, professional help.

Create a Physically and Emotionally Safe Space

A person in a trauma response often operates from a place of fear and a shattered sense of security. Your first priority is to help them feel safe.

- **Be a Gentle Representative of Jesus:** A trauma survivor's nervous system is hypersensitive to perceived threats. Counteract this by being consistently gentle, reassuring, and affirming.

- **Embrace the Ministry of Presence:** Often, the best ministry is simply showing up, listening deeply, and being a compassionate, calm presence. Your consistent, non-anxious presence can help soothe their nervous system.

- **Beware of Religious Triggers:** Recognize that many trauma survivors have been hurt by religious people or institutions. Some spiritual practices may feel overwhelming or triggering. Allow them to engage spiritually only to the degree they feel comfortable.

Listen with Empathy, not Judgment

A trauma survivor may feel an intense need to talk about what happened, or they may want to avoid the topic entirely. Your job is to be a good listener when they are ready.

- **Listen Without Agenda:** Let them speak their story without rushing them toward a happy ending or an immediate path to forgiveness. Don't feel you have to "fix" their problems.

- **Ask "What Happened to You?":** Shift your mindset from "What is wrong with you?" to "What happened to you?". This approach avoids judgment and validates their pain.

- **Validate Their Pain:** Instead of downplaying their feelings or comparing their struggles to others, offer validating statements.

"I am so sorry that happened to you."

"I can't imagine what that must have been like."

- **Avoid Platitudes:** Do not use phrases like "God has a plan" or "Everything happens for a reason" in the immediate aftermath of a trauma. Such statements can minimize their pain and damage trust.

Empower Them by Respecting Their Journey

Trauma can rob a person of their sense of choice and control. As you minister, help them regain a sense of empowerment.

- **Respect their Pace:** Healing is not linear and cannot be rushed. Be patient with setbacks and understand that recovery is a long-term process.

- **Help with Practical Needs:** Overwhelming circumstances can make even small tasks feel impossible. Offering specific, practical assistance (like a meal or helping with chores) is often a powerful form of care.

- **Encourage Professional Help:** Unless you are a licensed professional, do not offer counseling. Gently encourage them to seek a trained, licensed mental health professional who specializes in trauma. You can offer to help them find a suitable professional.

Care for Yourself as You Care for Others

Ministering to someone with trauma can be emotionally taxing. It is vital to care for your own well-being to avoid burnout and vicarious trauma.

- **Set Healthy Boundaries:** Know your limits and communicate them clearly. You are not responsible for carrying their burdens but for stewarding their story wisely and respectfully.

- **Have Your Own Support System:** Maintain your own network of friends and mentors. Supporting someone through trauma requires you to pour out, so you must also have people who pour back into you.

- **Take Care of Your Own Trauma:** If you are a trauma survivor yourself, recognize your own triggers and address them with a professional. Healing people who are hurt requires that you deal with your own pain

Creating a Ripple Effect: Restored People Restore People

The Restored people restore people is a powerful principle, deeply rooted in the Christian concept of restoration.

What it Means

When one person experiences profound healing or restoration through Christ, it creates a "ripple effect". That individual's transformation doesn't stop with them; it sends out waves of hope and grace to others.

By their actions and testimony, they can help guide others through their own brokenness, extending the same mercy and healing they received.

How it Works

- The initial healing: It starts with a broken person who allows God to do restorative work in their life.

- The healing spreads: That healing creates an inner overflow of joy, grace, and empathy that naturally touches others around them.

- Purposeful ministry: This leads to a life of intentional service, using your own healed story to help others on their path to restoration

Scripture Anchor: *"They overcame him by the blood of the Lamb and by the word of their testimony." (Revelation 12:11).*

Chapter 9

LIVING IN DIVINE OR BECOMING YOUR BEST SELF IN CHRIST WITH THE HOLY SPIRIT

Declare God's way as your way, and His timing as your timing. It is the prophetic shift from chasing outcomes in chaos to trusting the God who brings peace. Let go of your need to control the timeline and watch everything fall into place as His perfect plan unfolds".

Walking Daily in God's Structure: Prayer, Obedience, Discernment

Walking daily in God's structure is that it leads to peace instead of chaos. This happens through a continuous, three-step cycle:

- **Prayer:** You start the day in conversation with God to set the pace, surrendering your will to His.

- **Obedience:** Your alignment with God's will translates into action. This daily decision to follow His lead builds faithfulness and brings blessings.

- **Discernment:** Your habit of prayer and obedience sharpens your ability to hear God's voice and see His hand at work, guiding you to distinguish between His way and the ways of the world. actively resisting sin and temptation to prevent spiritual attack. You close these doors by aligning your life with God's will and quickly addressing sin.

Keeping Doors Closed to the Enemy

How to Keep Doors Closed

1. **Repentance:** Confess and turn away from sin immediately. This closes doors opened by disobedience.

2. **Resistance:** Actively resist temptation and rebuke the enemy's whispers, replacing lies with God's truth.

3. **Forgiveness:** Refuse to harbor bitterness or unforgiveness, which can give the enemy a foothold in your heart.

4. **Rest:** Recognize that exhaustion and burnout create spiritual vulnerability. Rest without guilt and rebuild your strength through spiritual renewal.

5. **Vigilance:** Remain alert and watchful in prayer, guarding what you allow into your mind and spirit

Maintaining Healing: Ongoing Deliverance and Spiritual Growth

Maintaining healing is an active, ongoing lifestyle, not a one-time event. To stay free and keep spiritual momentum, you must daily replace old patterns with intentional, God-centered habits.

To Maintain Healing

1. **Stay in the Word:** Fill your mind with God's truth to counter the enemy's lies and worldly thinking.

2. **Worship and pray daily:** Use praise as a spiritual weapon and maintain consistent connection with God.

3. **Confess and repent quickly:** Immediately address any new or returning sin that could open a door to spiritual oppression.

4. **Guard your "gates":** Be mindful of the media you consume, protecting what enters your mind and spirit.

5. **Build a community:** Connect with a healthy church and have trusted spiritual mentors for prayer and accountability

Daily Habits of Victorious Living

Here are some short and sweet daily habits for a victorious life:

1. **Start with Truth:** Begin your day in God's Word to align your perspective with His promises.

2. **Pray Without Ceasing:** Maintain a constant conversation with God, bringing every concern and victory to Him throughout the day.

3. **Worship Daily:** Use praise and worship to combat spiritual heaviness and create an atmosphere for God's presence.

4. **Stay Accountable:** Live in community with other believers for support, prayer, and encouragement.

5. **Guard Your Gates:** Protect what enters your mind and spirit, filtering out negativity and focusing on what is pure.

6. **Repent Quickly:** Maintain a pure heart by confessing and turning from sin as soon as you recognize it.

Scripture Anchor: *"Seek first the kingdom of God and His righteousness, and all these things shall be added to you." (Matthew 6:33).*

CONCLUSION

Rising Above for God's Glory

Your story of rising above is a testament to God's power and grace. It's a purposeful narrative that transforms your pain into ministry, restoring others because you were restored. By living in divine order, maintaining your healing, and following daily habits of victorious living, you declare that your best self is your God-self. In doing so, your life becomes a ripple effect of God's love, bringing Him glory and hope to a hurting world.

Final Encouragement

Your Trauma does NOT define You, Your Restoration Does. Your trauma is part of your story, but it is not your final chapter. Your willingness to heal is what truly defines you.

Prophetic Declaration Over Your Life

Divine restoration is yours. Your future is filled with peace and purpose. You are equipped with strength and power for every obstacle. Abundant favor and blessing are coming to you.

Closing prayer of Healing, Deliverance, and Restoration

Father, Son, Holy-Spirit we thank you for your constant presence and unending love. We pray for your healing grace to touch every broken place, for your deliverance to set us free from all that holds us captive, and for your divine restoration to make us whole again. May our hearts, minds, and souls be renewed by your power. In your holy name, in Christ Jesus name Amen.

Call to Action: Rise Up, Walk in Divine Order, and Help Others Find Freedom

Rise up and claim your divine order. As you walk in freedom, use your liberty to lift others out of captivity.

From Breaking Chains to Divine Order: A Prophetess Guide to Healing, Freedom, and Power in Christ Jesus Name

PROPHETIC PRAYERS FOR EACH CHAPTER

Introduction Prayer

"Father, I thank You for every person who holds this book in their hands. I decree and declare that as they read, the Spirit of the Lord will break chains, open eyes, and stir up faith for restoration. Lord, breathe upon these words and let them be life to the weary, healing to the broken, and strength to the weak. In Jesus' mighty name, Amen."

Chapter 1: The Wounds We Carry

"Lord, I bring every hidden wound, every scar from childhood, into Your presence. I declare that no pain will remain buried, but will be brought into the light of Your healing love. Father, touch every place in my heart that has been broken, and begin the work of restoration today. Amen."

Chapter 2: The Enemy's Trap

"By the authority of Jesus Christ, I cancel every assignment of the enemy that has tried to bind me through trauma. I break cycles of fear, rejection, and shame. I declare that every trap of darkness is exposed and destroyed by the light of Christ. No weapon formed against me shall prosper. Amen."

Chapter 3: The Lie of Staying Broken

"Father, uproot every lie I have believed about myself. Silence the voice of the enemy that says I am not enough, I am too damaged, or I will never change. I declare the truth: I am a child of God, chosen, loved, and restored. Amen."

Chapter 4: God, the Only True Restorer

"Lord, I thank You that You are the God of restoration. I declare that You are restoring my heart, my mind, my body, and my spirit. I speak Joel 2:25 over my life: every year the enemy has stolen shall be returned in greater measure. Amen."

Chapter 5: Power Over Darkness

"In the name of Jesus, I bind every demonic spirit that has sought to oppress me through trauma. I command witches, warlocks, and workers of darkness to flee. I put on the full armor of God and declare victory over every spiritual battle. The blood of Jesus covers me and speaks better things over my life. Amen."

Chapter 6: The Path of Healing

"Father, walk me step by step through the process of healing. Give me the grace to forgive, the strength to let go, and the courage to embrace wholeness. I declare that I am being transformed by the renewing of my mind, and I will not return to the old ways. Amen."

Chapter 7: Becoming Your Best Self in Christ

"Lord, reveal my true identity in You. Show me the purpose You created me for. I declare that I will rise above the ashes of trauma and step into the beauty of my divine calling. I am confident, bold, and strong in the Lord. Amen."

Chapter 8: Helping Others Heal

"Father, use my testimony as a weapon of deliverance for others. Anoint my words, my story, and my life to bring freedom to the captives. I declare that my healing will overflow to my family, my community, and generations after me. Amen."

Chapter 9: Living in Divine Order

"Lord, establish Your order in my life. Remove every distraction, every open door to the enemy, and every weight that slows me down. I declare that I will seek first Your kingdom, and everything else will align according to Your divine plan. Amen."

Closing Prayer

"Heavenly Father, I thank You for restoration, healing, and freedom. I seal every word of this book with the blood of Jesus. I declare over my life and the lives of every reader: we are healed, we are whole, and we are rising up in divine order to give You glory. In Jesus' mighty and matchless name, Amen."

PROPHETIC DECLARATIONS FOR EACH CHAPTERS

Introduction Declaration

Father, Son and the Holy Spirit "I declare that this journey will change my life. God's Spirit is alive in me, and every chain will break as I walk through these pages."in Christ Jesus name.

Chapter 1: The Wounds We Carry

Father, Son and the Holy-Spirit "I declare that my wounds will no longer define me. My pain is being turned into purpose, and my scars are becoming testimonies of God's healing." in Christ Jesus name we pray.Hallelujah AMEN!."

Chapter 2: The Enemy's Trap

Father, Son and the Holy-Spirit "I declare that every trap of the enemy is broken in Jesus' name. I will not live in cycles of fear, rejection, or shame. I am free. in Christ Jesus name we pray.Hallelujah AMEN!."

Chapter 3: The Lie of Staying Broken

Father, Son and the Holy-Spirit "I declare that I am not broken beyond repair. I am whole in Christ. Every lie of the enemy is silenced, and the truth of God shapes my identity in Christ Jesus name we pray.Hallelujah AMEN!."

Chapter 4: God, the Only True Restorer

Father, Son and the Holy-Spirit "I declare that God is restoring everything I lost. My joy, my peace, my voice, and my purpose are being made new by His hand in Christ Jesus name we pray. Hallelujah AMEN!."

Chapter 5: Power Over Darkness

Father, Son and the Holy-Spirit "I declare that no witch, warlock, or demonic force has power over me. I walk in divine authority, and the blood of Jesus covers and protects me in Christ Jesus name we pray. Hallelujah AMEN!."

Chapter 6: The Pat h of Healing

Father, Son and the Holy-Spirit "I declare that I will walk boldly through the process of healing. I will forgive, release, and step into wholeness. My mind is renewed daily. in Christ Jesus name we pray. Hallelujah AMEN!."

Chapter 7: Becoming Your Best Self in Christ

Father, Son and the Holy-Spirit "I declare that I am everything God says I am: chosen, loved, anointed, and powerful. I am rising into my best self through Christ." in Christ Jesus name we pray. Hallelujah AMEN!."

Chapter 8: Helping Others Heal

Father, Son and the Holy-Spirit "I declare that my testimony is a weapon. My healing will set others free, and I am a vessel of deliverance in God's hands in Christ Jesus name we pray.Hallelujah AMEN!."

Chapter 9: Living in Divine Order

Father, Son and the Holy-Spirit "I declare that my life is aligned with God's divine order. I walk in obedience, I live in victory, and I move in God's perfect timing in Christ Jesus name we pray.Hallelujah AMEN!."

Closing Declaration

Father, Son and the Holy-Spirit "I declare that I am free, I am whole, and I am rising above for God's glory. My past will not hold me, my trauma will not define me, and my future is secure in Christ Jesus name we pray.Hallelujah AMEN!."

From Breaking Chains to Divine Order: A Prophetess Guide to Healing, Freedom, and Power in Christ Jesus Name

REFLECTION & JOURNALING EXERCISE FOR EACH CHAPTERS

Introduction Exercise

- Write down what you hope to gain from reading this book.

- Ask yourself: What areas of my life do I want God to restore?

Chapter 1: The Wounds We Carry

- List 2–3 painful childhood experiences that still affect you today.

- Write a letter (you don't have to send it) to your younger self, offering compassion and acknowledging the pain.

Chapter 2: The Enemy's Trap

- Identify any negative cycles or patterns in your life (fear, rejection, anger, broken relationships).

- Reflect: Where do I see the enemy trying to use my trauma against me?

Chapter 3: The Lie of Staying Broken

- Write down the lies you've believed about yourself (e.g., "I am not worthy," "I will always be broken").

- On the opposite side, write God's truth from scripture that cancels that lie.

Chapter 4: God, the Only True Restorer

- Journal about a time God restored something in your life, even if small

- Write a prayer asking God to restore specific areas (relationships, confidence, peace, etc.).

Chapter 5: Power Over Darkness

- Reflect: Have you ever felt spiritual resistance or oppression? Write about it.

- Write out a declaration using your own words: "In Jesus' name, I break… [name specific fear, curse, or attack]."

Chapter 6: The Pat h of Healing

- Make a forgiveness list: write the names of those who hurt you. (You don't have to forgive all at once, but start with one name.)

- Journal: How does it feel when I imagine letting this pain go?

Chapter 7: Becoming Your Best Self in Christ

- Write down 5 qualities you believe God placed in you (strength, creativity, wisdom, compassion, etc.).

- Write a vision statement: Who is my best self in Christ?

Chapter 8: Helping Others Heal

- Reflect on someone in your life who needs encouragement. Write what you would say to them if you were ministering from your healing.

- Journal: How can my testimony be used to lift others?

Chapter 9: Living in Divine Order

- Write a daily schedule that puts God first (prayer, Word, worship).

- Journal: What distractions or habits do I need to remove to live in God's order?

Closing Exercise

- Write a final declaration: "This is who I was. This is who I am now. This is who I will be in Christ."

THANKSGIVING PRAYER

Father,Son,Holy Spirit thank you for who I was, who I am now and who I will be in Christ. My past has passed, my present is dwelling in your presence and my future is already in your hands in Christ Jesus name we pray. Hallelujah AMEN!

Prophetic Prayer

Father,Son, HOLY-Spirit I bring every hidden wound into Your light. I declare that my heart is being restored by Your power in Christ Jesus name we pray...Hallelujah Amen

Prophetic Declarations

- *I declare my wounds no longer define me.*
- *I declare my scars will become my testimony.*
- *I declare I am healed and restored in Christ.*

Reflection & Journaling Exercise

- Write down 2–3 painful experiences that shaped you.
- What lies did the enemy tell you because of those experiences? What does God say about you instead?

Action Step

"Choose one wound from your past and write a prayer asking God to begin healing that area this week."

Listen, we know your pain was real, but your healing will be greater. You are stepping into a new chapter of your story in Christ Jesus' name.

From Breaking Chains to Divine Order: A Prophetess Guide to Healing, Freedom, and Power in Christ Jesus Name.

Hey its Lakay Liline Ministries Domestic Industies! Lakay Liline Ministries Private and Personal Chef Services and we are praying with YOU! Delivering Kingdom Business what to the what what what.. PERIOD IN CHRIST JESUS NAME! Sounds Familiar?

My name is Sherline Oscar-Marcellus and I want to thank you personally for reading and buying our book! As a mother of two autistic children, a wife, and a prayer warrior, I wrote From Breaking Chains to Divine Order: A Prophetess Guide to Healing, Freedom, and Power in Christ Jesus Name to be A Guide to Healing, Freedom, and Restoration because I never had a guide for my own battles. I've learned that our struggles are not against people, but against spiritual forces that try to block our destiny.

Between running businesses, and caring for my family, I found healing and freedom through the power of The Father,Son and Holy-Spirit. This book carries my heart, my faith, and the lessons I've lived and walked through. It's for anyone who needs to know that the BLOOD can RESTORE, HEAL, and SET YOU FREE no matter what you face.

www.ingramcontent.com/pod-product-compliance
Lightning Source LLC
Chambersburg PA
CBHW070201100426
42743CB00013B/3004